THE BODY YOU LEFT BEHIND

YOUR 5-STEP BODY PARTNERSHIP FRAMEWORK

A Practical Guide to Rebuild Trust in Your Body and Reclaim your Life

Dr Valerie Johnston-Dugamin

Copyright © 2025 Dr Valerie Johnston-Dugamin

All rights reserved.

No part of this publication may be reproduced, distributed, or transmitted in any form or by any means, including photocopying, recording, or other electronic or mechanical methods, without the prior written permission of the publisher, except in the case of brief quotations embodied in critical reviews and certain other non-commercial uses permitted by copyright law.

For permission requests, write to the publisher at:

info@osteolife.com.au

ISBN: 978-1-7641660-0-3 (paperback)
ISBN: 978-1-7641660-1-0 (ebook)
Cover design by: Olagunju Haadi
Printed in Australia

Disclaimer

This book is intended for informational and educational purposes only. It is not a substitute for professional medical advice, diagnosis, or treatment. Always seek the advice of your physician or other qualified health provider with any questions you may have regarding a medical condition.

The author and publisher disclaim any liability for any adverse effects resulting directly or indirectly from the information contained in this book. Reliance on any information provided herein is solely at your own risk.

Acknowledgments

To my incredible clients,

Thank you for trusting me with your bodies and stories. Your courage to be seen, heal, and grow inspires me deeply. This book carries pieces of your journeys a responsibility I hold with immense gratitude.

To my family and friends,

Your unwavering support and encouragement gave me strength when the path was uncertain and reminded me why this work matters.

To my coaches and mentors,

Thank you for challenging and guiding me, shaping both this book and the woman I am today.

To Serena Williams,

Thank you for showing what it means to rise again – with courage, spirit, and unwavering strength.

And to my body,

You have carried me through every season, spoken truths even when ignored, and always brought me home. I owe this book – and so much more – to you.

With profound gratitude,

— Dr. Valerie Johnston-Dugamin

About the author

Dr. Valerie Johnston-Dugamin is a Doctor of Osteopathy and creator of the OsteoLife LUCKY System™, a practical, experience-based 5-step framework developed from thousands of clinical hours and patient experiences. Drawing on decades of clinical work, she helps people reconnect with their bodies and regain balance.

Valerie's approach is grounded in the understanding that your body is not a problem to solve, it's a place to come home to. Through this compassionate perspective, she invites readers to realign with their bodies, supporting energy, clarity, and lasting wellbeing in today's fast-paced world.

Contents

Preface	vi
Introduction	x
Chapter 1 – Disconnection	xii
Chapter 2 – Listen	26
Chapter 3 – Understand	46
Chapter 4 – Connecting	76
Chapter 5 – Kindness	99
Chapter 6 – You take action	117
Chapter 7 – Leading from alignment	135
Final Reflection	151
Toolkit + next steps	154
OsteoLife LUCKY Toolkit worksheets	158

Preface

The Body You Left Behind didn't begin with a concept. It began with silence.

Not the kind that soothes, but the kind that signals disconnection. The kind that settles in when your voice becomes unfamiliar, and your body feels like a stranger. When competence becomes your armour to hide fatigue.

When people see your achievements but not your struggle.

I lived that. For years I built, delivered, cared, and produced. I gave to clients, family, and my business… until there was nothing left to give to myself. I wasn't unwell. I was functioning, admired, and even thriving on the surface. But underneath I was absent from my own experience.

What I've learnt, both personally and professionally, is this: you can abandon your body without ever leaving your home, your job, or your relationships.

My own reckoning came in 2017, when my body finally said no. What looked like strength on the outside was, in reality, chronic override. It took burnout, stillness, and two months of forced recovery to realise I hadn't truly checked in with myself in years.

I wasn't looking to create a system, but that's what emerged. I was just trying to survive. But slowly, through reflection, listening, and relearning how to inhabit my own body, a rhythm began to form. A process. A way back. I didn't have a name for it then, but I do now.

You'll meet it soon. It's called the OsteoLife LUCKY System™.

You can meet every external demand, yet slowly disconnect from yourself. In over 12 years as an osteopath, working hands-on with thousands of clients, I've witnessed this story in every kind of body: business owners, caregivers, athletes, parents, performers, educators, builders, and creatives.

Many came to me not because something was *wrong*, but because something no longer felt *right*.

They were tired in ways sleep didn't touch.

They felt disconnected, unanchored, and out of rhythm with themselves.

They longed for a version of themselves they couldn't name, but instinctively missed.

What they were really missing... was their body. Not the shape of it. Not some 'before' version, but the intelligence, the presence, the innate wisdom that had once guided them and had gradually been overwritten by stress, speed, and survival mode.

This book is not a fix. It's a return.

It won't give you a five-step plan to 'get your body back', because you never lost it. You just stopped listening.

It's a guided return, or a map home. Not to the body you had, but to the body that's been waiting for you all along.

Each chapter follows the rhythm of the OsteoLife LUCKY System, the same framework I use in my clinic and programs.

Listen

Understand

Connect

Kindness

You take action

It's a framework rooted in over a decade of clinical practice – shaped by real conversations, real bodies, and the raw, unfiltered wisdom that only hands-on experience can teach. It guides you through a practical, compassionate shift from managing your body to actually partnering with it.

In this book you will find stories – mine and those of real clients – reflections, gentle prompts, and embodied practices.

Not to *fix* you, but to help you *find* you. To bring you back to the body you left behind – or perhaps were never fully taught to trust in the first place.

This book was written in the in-between spaces: before my clinic sessions, after clients, and in quiet weekend mornings.

I didn't write it because I had time. I wrote it because I ran out of reasons not to.

You won't find shame here. You won't find judgement.

You'll find warmth, clarity, and above all, an invitation.

Not to go back. But to go deeper.

Not to fix. But to remember who you are when your body is included, respected, and heard.

Welcome home.

Let's begin by understanding what disconnection really looks like – not as a concept, but as a quiet pattern that unfolds over time.

You may not realise how far you've drifted until something inside you starts to whisper: 'There must be more than this.'

The Introduction is your first step towards remembering – not just *why* you left your body behind… but *how* to finally come back on your own terms.

Introduction

This book is about understanding your body's needs, not about what *you* think it needs. It's about presence, and the moment you began managing your body instead of inhabiting it – not with intention, but with survival. You judged, controlled, ignored, suppressed, and overrode what your body tried to say. Now it is time to listen.

As a health practitioner working in the allied health and the somatic wellness space, I've seen this pattern in hundreds of high-functioning individuals.

The people I have worked with did not fail at life. They succeeded at it – often too well. Yet that success sometimes comes with a cost: a gradual drifting away from self.

They hadn't abandoned their responsibilities. They had simply detached from themselves.

Not by choice. Not overnight. But over years of perfectionism, over-giving, hyper-productivity, and unspoken trauma.

That's what this book explores: not how to fix your body, but how to return to it. Not to a previous version of yourself, but to the one that is here now. A return that is sensory, emotional, grounded, and deeply respectful.

My process is not only theoretical. It emerged through clinical practice – thousands of hours of listening to real people, with real stories, through real, hands-on work. From that, I developed a rhythm, a system that helps people come home to their bodies in a way that lasts.

It's called the OsteoLife LUCKY System – a five-phase process built on Listening, Understanding, Connection, Kindness, and Your Next Action. It is not a quick fix. It's a reconnection – one that unfolds gently, one layer at a time.

You'll meet this framework throughout the book, but it isn't there to give you rules – it's there to give you rhythm.

Each chapter builds on a structure that mirrors the return to your body: Definition, Why, When, Where, How, My experience, Real stories, What changed, Lessons learnt, Try this today, Pause and reflect, and Invitation.

These aren't just headers. They reflect the way transformation can happen. Not in a straight line, but in cycles.

The stories in this book, mine and those of my clients, are not meant to inspire from a distance. They are there to sit beside you, to show you that disengagement isn't the end of the story, and that return is not only possible, but natural.

Somewhere in these pages you'll see yourself. Not the version others applaud, but the version you long to feel again.

The OsteoLife LUCKY System becomes your tool – not to perform for the world, but to reunite with your own body as it is.

Each step builds on the one before it. Each step invites a small shift – one you can feel, not just understand.

I've seen again and again that awareness alone doesn't change anything. Reconnection needs rhythm. It needs something steady, simple, and embodied, something that holds you when the old patterns try to pull you back.

That's what this framework offers. Not a prescription. Not a plan to fix you. But a path – reliable, flexible, grounded – that leads you back to your body.

The OsteoLife LUCKY System is here to meet you exactly where you are and guide you home, one small, powerful step at a time.

But before we begin, there's one truth we can't skip: you left your body behind. And it's time to understand why.

CHAPTER 1

Disconnection

> *When you left your body without realising it – and how to begin coming home.*

What is disconnection

That silent detachment is not just a mental state – it's a physiological silence. It's what happens when your body shifts from being a partner to being a project. You stop living in it and start managing it.

You override hunger, ignore exhaustion, suppress emotions, and power through. You live from the neck up – producing, solving, fixing – while your body becomes something you tolerate, criticise, or control. You still function, but you don't feel.

And, slowly, you stop trusting the very vessel that carries you.

Why do we disconnect?

We disconnect because disconnection is rewarded.

We are praised for being productive, admired for self-control, and respected for pushing through. From a young age we are taught that rest is lazy, that feeling is weakness, and that thinness is worth more than satisfaction. We are trained to perform.

We internalise the messages that our body must be disciplined, sculpted, improved, and silenced. Until, eventually, we no longer recognise this drift as a problem, because it wears the mask of success.

But, inside, something feels off-balance. Empty, silent, unfamiliar.

When does disconnection show up?

Disconnection rarely arrives in a single moment.

It begins early, often in adolescence, when your body begins to change and the world starts commenting on it. It deepens through emotional neglect, trauma, control, or the pressure to perform.

It escalates in adulthood – through burnout, caregiving, parenting, or overachieving. It may show up postpartum, after illness, or during life transitions where your body feels functional, but unfamiliar.

You don't always notice when it starts – but you know when it's there.

You feel the absence. The numbness. The sense of being inside your life, but outside yourself.

Where is disconnection felt?

You feel it in your mornings when you rush, skip breakfast, and call it discipline.
You feel it in workouts that punish instead of nourish.

You see it in mirrors you avoid and wardrobes that never feel quite right.
It shows up at mealtime, when guilt replaces pleasure.
It echoes in social media scrolls, where comparison feeds shame.
It's hidden in your language, when you say, 'I don't have time', or 'I just need to get through this week'.
It's in the way you always give, perform, and push, but rarely pause to ask, 'How do I actually feel?'

My experience

For a long time I believed I was doing everything right. I exercised regularly, ate well, prioritised sleep, and pursued personal growth. On paper I was taking care of myself. I believed that because I had healthy habits, I must be in a healthy relationship with my body.

But things began to shift when I moved to Australia. I had to communicate in another language and learn a new culture. Life was at a new pace. I enrolled at university, studying in English. Then came work as an osteopath, and eventually the business I had always dreamed of – my own practice, where I gave everything to my clients and demanded excellence from myself.

I pushed forward with discipline, drive, and a deep desire to succeed. I completed professional development courses, ran a growing clinic, and showed up for others without fail. And all the while I never paused to ask: How is my body coping with all this?

In 2017 it caught up with me.

My body stopped. It didn't whisper; it collapsed. Two months of forced stillness followed – a time where recovery became my only job. That experience changed me. Not because I realised that I had done everything wrong, but because I realised I had done everything *without checking in.*

And like any place you check in to, your body needs to be acknowledged. You don't walk into a hotel and just assume there's space for you – you check in. You ask. You get the keys. You honour the threshold.

The body works the same way. When we rush past that moment of checking in, we miss the truth of whether there's capacity, whether rest is needed, whether it's already stretched thin.

From that moment forward my relationship with my body changed. I stopped assuming I knew what it needed. I began asking and listening. I tracked how unplanned events, grief, tension, or pressure registered in my system.

I still have ambition, but I now live it in partnership with my body, not at its expense.

That's where reconnection began for me – not in a dramatic transformation, but in a subtle powerful shift: the decision to stop assuming and start listening.

What I discovered in my own journey wasn't unique. Again and again I've seen the same turning point in others – not when life got easier, or time magically appeared, but when they chose to stop abandoning their bodies and started listening.

Real stories – the shift starts small

These stories aren't about perfection. They're about permission. Real people. Real resistance. And the moment they chose to reconnect.

What did they all have in common? They stopped overriding their body's signal, and they started paying attention.

These are just a few of their stories. They are not perfect. Or linear. But they are real.

Let them remind you that reconnection is possible. And it starts exactly from where you are.

When busyness replaces presence – and the body starts to disappear

Pam, 45, was a high-level executive in the finance sector, known for her sharp mind and relentless pace. She had climbed the ladder with precision and power – but at a cost no one could see.

When she first came to see me, she didn't talk about emotions. She talked about performance: missed meetings due to migraines, unpredictable digestion, and mounting fatigue that even her morning espresso ritual couldn't override.

'I don't have time for this,' she said, half-apologetically, half-defiantly. 'I need my body to get on board. I've got things to do.'

For three years she hadn't eaten a single meal sitting down. Lunch was fuel, not nourishment – usually protein bars between calls or takeaways consumed while answering emails. Her days were full, her calendar colour-coded and optimised. But her body? It had become background noise.

She wasn't broken. She was efficient and high-functioning. But underneath it all she was profoundly detached.

When I gently asked her when she had last paused just to notice how she felt, she blinked. 'I don't do that,' she said. 'If I stop, I'll fall behind.'

We didn't start with food, supplements, or posture. We started with space.

Her first practice was deceptively simple: take one lunch break outdoors. No phone. No screen. Just her, a real meal, and time.

She said that the first time felt 'pointless'. The second time she noticed her jaw unclenching. And by the end of the week something had shifted – not just in her digestion, which had already improved, but in how she *felt* in her body.

'I forgot I had a body,' she whispered during our third session, her eyes misting. 'I've spent years pushing it around. I never stopped to just... be in it.'

As she continued creating micro-moments of connection – breathing before meetings, pausing before reacting – her migraines decreased. Her tension softened. But the most profound change wasn't physical.

She began to speak about herself with more compassion. She started asking, 'What does my body need?' instead of, 'How do I make this go away?'

Her team noticed. One colleague said to her, 'You seem... different. Like you're not at war with yourself anymore.'

When I asked her what changed, she said: 'I used to treat my body like an assistant. Now I treat it like a partner. It shows up for me every day. It's about time I showed up for it.'

What changed for Pam?

- Pam recognised that her symptoms weren't failures – they were signals.
- She created micro-pauses to reconnect instead of waiting for a breakdown.
- She began to lead her body, not override it.

Lessons learnt

- You don't need a crisis to reclaim your body.
- Productivity without presence is a form of self-abandonment.
- Small acts of noticing can rebuild deep trust.

How is Pam now?

Pam still eats lunch outside three times a week – sometimes alone, sometimes with a colleague she trusts. She starts every Monday with a 60-second check-in before opening her laptop. Her migraines haven't disappeared entirely, but they've become less frequent – and less frightening. Most importantly, she no longer waits for her body to scream before she listens.

She doesn't see this as self-care. She sees it as leadership.

When rest felt indulgent – until it became essential

Robyn was a mother of three, running her household with military precision. Her calendar was packed with appointments, school runs, sports practice, and everyone else's needs. Her own body? Always last on the list. Sleep was fragmented. Meals were rushed. Movement was functional, never nourishing.

She wore exhaustion like a badge of honour. 'I'm just tired,' she would say, brushing off the persistent headaches, the racing mind, the quiet resentment building in her chest. She believed fatigue was the tax she had to pay for being a good mother.

Our first conversation wasn't about pain points. It was about permission. I asked, 'What would happen if rest wasn't failure, but leadership?'

That question shifted something.

She began by adding a 15-minute 'no doing' block each day. No multitasking. No catch-up. No guilt. Just presence.

At first, it felt uncomfortable – like a stolen moment she hadn't earned. But slowly she started to soften.

The headaches eased. The edge in her voice relaxed. She became less reactive with her children, more available to her partner, and – most importantly – more connected to herself. The rest of her routine remained intact, but her relationship with her body changed. She no longer saw her limits as flaws. She saw them as signals.

What changed for Robyn?

- She reframed rest from luxury to leadership.
- She stopped apologising for her own capacity.
- She discovered that small pauses could restore big energy.

Lessons learnt

- You don't need a full day off to come back to yourself.
- Rest is not a break from responsibility – it's a return to it.
- Softness is not weakness. It's a recalibration of strength.

How is Robyn now?

Robyn's 'no doing' blocks are still in her calendar – and they are non-negotiable. Her family knows that this time matters – not because she's unavailable, but because she's choosing to be present afterwards. She no longer chases balance. She creates space. One pause at a time.

What changed for Pam and Robyn?

It wasn't their routine. It was their relationship with their body.

Neither of them overhauled their life. They made one conscious shift: they stopped treating their bodies like problems to fix – and started treating them like partners to lead with. They moved from silent survival to conscious connection.

The transformation wasn't just physical. It was relational.

They didn't do more. They did less – with more intention.

And that made all the difference.

Now, it's your turn.

Try this today – the evening check-in

Before going to bed tonight, pause.
Don't try to fix anything. Don't be optimistic. Don't scroll.
Just sit quietly, even for 60 seconds.

Ask yourself:
- Did I feel present in my body today?
- When did I override it, push past it, or ignore it?
- What did I need, but didn't give?

You don't need to journal, and there is no perfect answer. Just honesty.

Noticing is enough.

Pause and reflect

Where in your day did you disconnect from yourself?
What moments did your body whisper discomfort – and you overrode it?
What belief tells you that slowing down means falling behind?
What might shift if you stopped managing your body – and started listening to it?

Invitation

Are you ready for the transformation?

You don't have to earn your return. You don't need to hit rock bottom.

You are allowed to come back to your body now – exactly as you are. One breath, one pause, one honest check-in at a time. That's how reconnection begins. Quietly. Not with a breakthrough, but with a shift.

And yet, awareness alone isn't enough. Many of my clients were already aware something was off. They had tried everything – diets, doctors, gym memberships, meditation apps, or wellness retreats. Each brought temporary relief, but not lasting reconnection. Not because they lacked discipline, but because effort isn't the solution.

What's needed isn't more doing.
What's needed is a new way of relating:
Understanding, not urgency.
Compassion, not control.
Structure, without rigidity.

Next step

Now you have seen the cost of this quiet withdrawal. And how it hides in high-functioning lives, how it distances you from your own experience, and how it makes you go through the motions instead of really being there.

But this drift is not your flaw. It's your signal.
It is not the end. It is the entry point.

What you felt in this chapter wasn't just recognition – it was readiness. The quiet acknowledgment that this pace, this pressure, this distance… is no longer sustainable.

You're not here because you're broken. You're here because you're done surviving.

What follows is the pathway forward.
Your return starts here with the OsteoLife LUCKY System.
This isn't a theory. It's practice.

It was developed in a clinical setting and refined through real lives. It was tested in the aftermath of burnout, disconnection, and uncertainty.

It's simple, it's rhythmic, and it works – not by force, but by trust.
Each chapter from here on guides you through one phase of reconnection:

L – Listen	Reconnection begins by hearing the messages beneath your symptoms.
U – Understand	Awareness becomes clarity when you release judgement.
C – Connect	Presence is the foundation of every relationship – including the one with yourself.
K – Kindness	True change lasts only when it's rooted in safety, not shame.
Y – You Take Action	Embodiment is not a concept – it's a daily commitment.

These aren't just steps – they are your rhythm of return.
You don't need to rush, and you don't need to master it all at once.

You just need to begin.

We begin with L – Listen.

CHAPTER 2

Listen

> *Your body has been talking. Are you finally ready to hear it?*

What is listening?

What does it mean to listen?

Listening is the moment you stop overriding and start noticing. It's the embodied, intentional practice of tuning into your body's quiet signals – *before* they become demands.

Most people wait until pain forces them to stop. But the body rarely begins with a scream. It begins with a whisper: a clench in the jaw, a flutter in the gut, a heaviness behind the eyes. These are signals we've learnt to dismiss as 'normal', 'just stress', or 'nothing to worry about'.

But *familiar* doesn't mean *healthy*. And *coping* isn't the same as *connecting*.

To listen is to treat your body's subtle cues as meaningful, even when they seem small. It's to pause before reacting. To get curious instead of critical. And to let discomfort be a messenger, not a threat. Listening isn't about fixing what's wrong. It's about respecting what's real.

And when you practice that respect – consistently, gently, and without pressure – you begin to build trust. Not in theory, but in the felt, grounded experience of being in your body… without bracing against it.

Listening is the first return.

The first rhythm.

The first step towards home.

Why listening matters

Listening matters because your body always speaks first. Before your mind can name the overwhelm, your body has already noticed.

Your breath shortens.
Your jaw clenches.
Your chest tightens.
Your sleep shifts.

Long before burnout becomes visible, the body has pulled the handbrake – quietly, instinctively, and protectively.

But most of us are conditioned to override these early signals. We tell ourselves to push through, to keep performing, and to stay strong. We treat subtle discomfort as something to ignore… until it isn't subtle anymore.

If you miss the whisper, the body raises its voice.
That low hum of tension? It becomes chronic pain.
That unease in your gut? It becomes exhaustion.
That restlessness? It becomes disconnection.

Listening isn't indulgent – it's intelligent.

It's not about fragility – it's about foresight.
To listen is to lead – your energy, your boundaries, and your recovery.
It's not a passive practice. It's how you take authorship over your wellbeing, before your body is forced to take it back.

When to listen

Listen every day – especially at the times most people overlook.

Don't only listen during breakdowns or crises, but in the quiet transitions where your body whispers the truth:

Before you walk into a meeting.
After a tense conversation.
As you collapse onto the couch at night.

When you say 'I'm fine', but feel the opposite.
When something feels off and you don't have words for it yet.

These aren't throwaway moments – they're turning points in disguise.

Because, reconnection doesn't begin with grand gestures. It begins with presence in the in-between – when you're shifting roles, emotions, or expectations.

That pause you take before you react? That breath you notice before you respond?

That's the beginning of body fluency.
This is when to listen.
Not someday. Not when it's convenient.
But now – before the silence becomes too loud to ignore.

Where to listen

Listen anywhere you are willing to pause. You don't need a quiet retreat or perfect conditions.

You need a moment of presence:
- In your car, before you turn the ignition.
- At your desk, between back-to-back meetings.
- Standing at the sink, brushing your teeth.
- Lying in bed, five minutes before sleep.
- In the bathroom, away from the noise.
- In line at the supermarket, while you wait your turn.

The location doesn't matter. Your willingness does.

Reconnection isn't a performance. It's a pattern – one that begins when you choose to be with yourself, not to manage yourself.

How to start listening

The **TUNE-IN Map**™ is a tool to help you listen to your body – not to fix it, but to meet it.

It is a simple, repeatable way to reconnect with your body.
It isn't a performance tool. It's not something to master or perfect.
It's a practice of curiosity, honesty, and compassion.

The **TUNE-IN Map** was born not in theory, but of necessity – during a time when I looked healthy on paper but felt hollow inside. Despite years of 'doing the right things', I was still overriding my body in subtle but damaging ways.

I wasn't lazy. I wasn't broken.

I was disconnected.

The TUNE-IN Map became a turning point – not because it gave me control, but because it gave me a language.

A way to pause.
To listen.
To soften.
To stay.

And for my clients it's become a doorway – one that brings them back to themselves when everything else feels loud, confusing, or out of sync.

Whether you feel numb, tense, exhausted, or just unsure where to begin, this is your first step back. Not with pressure. But with presence.

My turning point

I didn't just develop the **TUNE-IN Map** from theory, but also from experience.

After graduating as an osteopath, I believed I had all the pieces in place. I knew the mechanics of the body. I understood healthy movement, alignment, and rehabilitation. I followed every prescribed habit – daily exercise, yoga, optimal nutrition, and sleep hygiene.

On paper I was the picture of wellness. But three years after opening my clinic, I burned out so severely I could barely function. I wasn't just tired – I was dismantled. And during those months of forced recovery, I couldn't hide behind knowledge or routines. I had nothing left but time and truth.

It hit me like a quiet shock: I had been doing everything *for* my body, but nothing *with* it. I was still powering through. Still overriding discomfort. Still relating to my body as something to manage, fix, or silence.

Every symptom – fatigue, anxiety, body aches – had been trying to communicate to me.

But I wasn't listening. I was assuming.
I wasn't observing. I was overriding.
I wasn't in a relationship with my body – I was in control.

That's when it changed.

Each morning I started with one simple act: I placed my hand on my chest and closed my eyes.

I asked myself: 'What is here right now?'

At first, the answer was always exhaustion.

But then, subtler signals began to emerge: a tightening in my stomach when I imagined returning to work. A heaviness in my chest when I thought of everything I had to hold. A shallow breath when I feared I might never feel like myself again.

It wasn't comfortable – but it was honest.

And for the first time, I understood: my body had been speaking to me all along.

I just hadn't learnt how to *tune in*.
That moment birthed what would become the **TUNE-IN Map**.
It is a simple structure for something most of us were never taught:
How to *feel*.

How to *listen*.

How to *meet ourselves* in real-time – without performance, judgement, or pressure.

Years later, during the COVID-19 pandemic, as the world slowed and many were thrust into stillness, I offered this process virtually to clients. It was meant to be supportive, and temporary.

But something deeper happened.

Clients who had been disconnected for decades started to feel again.

Some cried.
Some slept through the night for the first time in years.
Some said it felt like *coming home.*

That's when I knew – this wasn't just a practice.
It was a pathway.
A rhythm.
A way back to a relationship most of us didn't know we'd lost.

The TUNE-IN Map is not about control.
It's about connection.
And it begins exactly where you are – right here, right now.

The TUNE-IN Map wasn't designed as a clever acronym. It emerged from necessity, out of burnout, reflection, and eventually deep transformation.

But each letter reflects one of the steps I had to learn, painfully and imperfectly.

Now, let's walk it together.

T – **Take 3 slow breaths** – I needed to learn to stop. To create space between me and my automatic reactions.

U – **Understand what I felt** – I'd spent years ignoring my sensations. I thought they were distractions. In fact, they were the information I needed most.

N – **Notice the location** – Finding a place of the feeling helped me see patterns I'd never noticed before.

E – **Explore the trigger** – I began to realise that symptoms often had context – the meeting that made me feel inadequate, the conversation that stirred old fears.

I – **Introduce myself to the emotion** – This was the hardest part: admitting I felt sadness or frustration felt like weakness. It was, in fact, the beginning of honesty.

N – **Notice my response** – I noticed that every time I suppressed an emotion, my body tensed further. Every time I acknowledged it, something softened.

This process didn't fix everything overnight. But it changed my relationship with my body from adversarial to collaborative. It stopped being an obstacle I needed to control, and started being a partner I could trust.

I didn't realise it at the time, but looking back, the foundations of what would later become the OsteoLife LUCKY System were already forming during my recovery in 2017.

Each shift I made – learning to listen, reflecting with kindness, and taking small intentional actions – wasn't just helping me heal. It was becoming a process. A rhythm. A way home.

I wasn't designing a method back then, I was surviving.

And over time the pattern revealed itself. What felt personal became transferable. What worked for me began to work for others. And that's when it began to take shape – slowly, organically, and powerfully. That shape would eventually become the TUNE-IN Map.

The TUNE-IN Map

Use this daily tool to help you reconnect with your body, gently, honestly, and without pressure.

T – Take 3 breaths	Slowly. Let yourself arrive in the moment.
U – Tune in to what you feel	Just try. Don't force. Stay curious.
N – Notice the location	Gentle observation. Where is it in your body?
E – Explore the trigger	Without judgement. What might have caused this?
I – Introduce yourself to the emotion	With kindness. You don't need to name it perfectly – just meet it.
N – Notice your response	Notice it with respect. How did you react or protect yourself?

Use this method daily – before bed, after a meeting, or any time you feel disconnected.

Even though the steps are simple, practising them isn't always easy. Most of us have spent years ignoring our signals or believing they were inconveniences to push past. Some people take to the TUNE-IN Map quickly. For others, it feels awkward, confronting, or even frustrating.

The TUNE-IN Map is also used in my workshops and client sessions to build daily body fluency. As you practice, this process becomes a personal language, one that helps you understand your body's messages with increasing clarity.

You don't have to master this map overnight. In fact, most people don't. Listening isn't about getting it right, it's about starting. It's about showing up, breath by breath, with a willingness to be present.

And you're not alone in this.

Real stories – listening in action

The stories that follow are real. They're the lived experiences of people who once felt just as unsure, disconnected, or sceptical as you might feel now. They didn't start with confidence, but they started with curiosity. They weren't seeking perfection – just a way to feel human again.

Their stories aren't here to inspire you from a distance. They're here to sit beside you, to remind you that even the smallest acts of listening can shift everything.

Let's begin with what listening looked like for them, so you can begin imagining what it might look like for you.

When pushing through stops working – and listening becomes survival

Clara, 39, was a senior executive at a fast-paced tech company. From the outside she had it all – a thriving career, a young family, and a beautiful home. But when she walked into my clinic her shoulders were nearly touching her ears. Her voice was tight and clipped as she rattled off the complaints she had rehearsed in her head: chronic migraines, jaw pain, and an ache between her shoulder blades that no amount of stretching or massage could relieve.

'I just need to fix this,' she said, almost apologetically, as if her pain was an inconvenience she was imposing on me. 'I can't keep losing days to these headaches. My team depends on me.'

Clara had spent years powering through. She didn't realise her body wasn't whispering anymore – it was screaming. She believed that if she just pushed harder, managed better, and ticked every box, the discomfort would disappear. But every week the symptoms grew louder.

She woke up exhausted. Her jaw was clenched so tightly that she had to physically pry it open each morning.

Underneath her frustration was quiet desperation. She didn't trust her body anymore. She felt betrayed – like it was sabotaging her success.

The first time I introduced her to the TUNE-IN Map, Clara looked sceptical. 'I don't have time to sit around feeling things,' she said, half laughing.

Still, she agreed to try it.

At our next session, she admitted she'd only practised it twice. 'It feels awkward,' she said. 'I sit there and… nothing happens.'

I reminded her: listening isn't about immediate insight. It's about making space.

In the second week something shifted. After a tense meeting where a client questioned her judgement, Clara noticed her temples throbbing. For the first time, she followed the TUNE-IN steps, hand trembling slightly.

'I feel dismissed,' she whispered.

Her body was telling the truth her mind had long suppressed.

Week by week, the connection grew clearer. Her migraines weren't random. They appeared every time she silenced herself, every time she traded authenticity for approval.

By the fourth week, she said something I'll never forget: **'My body isn't betraying me. It's protecting me. It's the only part of me that refuses to pretend.'**

That awareness shifted everything. She created a small ritual: she took five minutes each morning to breathe, check in, and write one honest sentence about what she felt. Within a month her migraines had dropped by half. And the pain in her shoulders no longer felt like a punishment – it felt like information.

But the real transformation wasn't physical. It was the way Clara began speaking about herself. She was steadier, softer. Her team noticed. One colleague even said, 'You seem different – in a good way. Like you're not carrying the weight of the world anymore.'

Today, Clara still uses the TUNE-IN Map. Not every day – but when that familiar tightness returns she knows not to override it.

When I asked her what changed, she smiled and said, 'I didn't fight my body this time. I listened to what it needed – instead of forcing what I thought it should want.'

What changed for Clara?

- She recognised her pain as a message, not a malfunction.
- She stopped equating output with value.
- She learnt to pause before reacting – so her body didn't have to escalate.

Lessons learnt

- Your body remembers what your mind tries to forget.
- Stillness can be an act of strength, not surrender.
- Listening is always the first step towards change.

How is Clara now?

Clara still begins most mornings with five quiet minutes to breathe, reflect, and write one line about how she feels. It's no longer a practice she 'makes time for' – it's part of how she leads.

Her migraines are rare now, and when they do come she no longer panics. She knows it's not failure. It's feedback.

She finally stopped seeing her body as an obstacle to overcome. She sees it as a compass, one that helps her lead with more clarity, communicate with more integrity, and live with more ease.

The high performer who managed everything – except herself

Sarah, 42, was a marketing director known for her composure under pressure. She was the one people called when deadlines collapsed, clients panicked, or entire projects derailed. She was dependable and unshakable. That was her identity.

But when she finally came to see me, her body was telling a different story.

Her shoulders were locked in a permanent brace. Her jaw ached every time she smiled. She woke each night at 3am, her heart racing and her mind spiralling through unfinished tasks and silent dread.

'It's just stress,' she said flatly, as if admitting anything deeper would be weakness.

When I asked how she managed it, she said, 'I power through.' Her voice cracked and her eyes filled. She blinked the tears away like she had a thousand times before. Holding it all together had become second nature – but it was costing her more than she realised.

When I introduced the TUNE-IN Map, she bristled. 'I don't see how naming my feelings helps,' she said. 'What good is all this sensation stuff? I need solutions, not emotions.'

Her resistance was honest and valid. She had spent her entire adult life operating on the belief that if you could just control the chaos, you could stay afloat.

But I reminded her: if you don't feel what's happening, you can't change it.

Her symptoms weren't the problem. They were the language her body had been speaking for years – she'd just never been taught how to listen.

She agreed, reluctantly, to try the TUNE-IN Map for seven days.

When she returned, she looked unsettled. 'I did it,' she said. 'And I realised… I don't actually know what I feel. Most of the time I'm either numb – or angry.'

That was her turning point.

She began to understand: the neck tension came from years of swallowing her needs. The headaches were the cost of pretending everything was fine. Her body wasn't the enemy; it was the messenger.

From then on, each morning before work she used the TUNE-IN Map. When her neck began to clench, she paused. She'd ask herself: 'What do I need right now?'

Sometimes the answer was simple – water, a walk, five quiet minutes. Sometimes it was harder – to say no, to delegate, to admit she was overwhelmed.

Bit by bit the tension softened. Her headaches eased. But more importantly, she stopped bracing against herself.

Her colleagues noticed too. One afternoon, a co-worker pulled her aside and said, 'You seem… lighter. Like you're finally breathing again.'

Months later, Sarah still uses the TUNE-IN Map. She keeps a small notebook on her desk, writing one sentence each morning about what she feels. A practice she once dismissed as pointless is now her daily anchor.

When I asked her what changed, she said, '**I stopped treating my body like a liability. I started treating it like a partner.**'

What changed for Sarah?

- She learnt that ignoring her body drained more energy than listening ever could.
- She stopped apologising for her needs and started respecting them.
- She replaced numbness with curiosity – and control with care.

Lessons learnt

- You can't change what you won't feel.
- Naming your truth doesn't weaken you – it frees you.
- Small acts of attention can lead to profound transformation.

How is Sarah now?

Sarah keeps her TUNE-IN notebook beside her laptop. It's her quiet ritual before each workday begins. She doesn't try to name every emotion perfectly – but she meets whatever's there with curiosity instead of judgement.

She still has intense weeks. But instead of bracing, she breathes. Instead of suppressing, she checks in.

What once felt like a foreign language – her body's signals – now feels like a conversation. And in that dialogue, Sarah has found something she never thought possible: steadiness without pretending, strength without tension, and success that doesn't cost her wellbeing.

Sarah's story reminds us that even if you start with resistance, you can still arrive at reconnection. Listening doesn't require perfection – only willingness

Try this today – the morning check-in

- Before the world reaches for you – before the emails, the headlines, the expectations – pause.
- Place a hand gently on your chest. Feel the rise and fall beneath your palm.
- Breathe in for four. Hold for four. Breathe out for four.
- Then ask yourself, softly but honestly: 'What do I feel in my body right now?'
- Don't analyse. Don't justify.
- Just notice.
- A flicker of tension. A wave of tiredness. A sense of calm you hadn't expected.
- Write down one sentence. That's it.

It may feel insignificant. But this is where reconnection begins – not in grand breakthroughs, but in 30-second moments of honesty.

Optional practice

- Set a gentle reminder for a midday pause. Take just 60 seconds to notice your breath, your posture, and your energy.

- Choose one everyday moment – like brushing your teeth or making tea – as your anchor. While you do it, ask: 'Is there anywhere in me that feels tight, numb, or overlooked?'

This is not about fixing.
It's about *noticing*.
Because listening is how your body learns that it matters.

Pause and reflect

Before you move forward, take a breath.

These questions aren't meant to be solved – they're meant to be felt.

1 – When was the last time your body whispered discomfort… and you kept going anyway?
What did you tell yourself in that moment?
And what did your body do next?

2 – What do you really believe about slowing down to listen?
Is it indulgent? Weak? Unproductive?
Whose voice shaped that belief?

3 – What signs does your body give you when you're close to feeling stressed or overwhelmed?
Is it through tight shoulders? Shallow breath? A rising sense of irritation or fatigue?

4 – What emotions surface when you imagine treating your body as a partner, not a problem?
Relief? Guilt? Resistance?
Let those feelings rise – they're part of the story too.

5 – Where in your day is there space to pause – even just for a moment?
You don't need an hour. You need intention. One window of stillness where listening is allowed.

TUNE-IN Map worksheet

Refer to the OsteoLife LUCKY Toolkit at the back of this book for the TUNE-IN Map worksheet.

Use it daily to:

- **Track** your body's signals – what you feel and where you feel it.
- **Identify** recurring triggers – moments, interactions, or thoughts that tighten your system.
- **Record** your most noticeable sensations – without judgement, just observation.

This isn't about doing it perfectly.

It's about building body fluency, one check-in at a time.

Chapter 2 tool recap

- **TUNE-IN Map** – Use this daily to notice and name your body's signals.
- **Morning check-in ritual** – Anchor your day with presence, not pressure.
- **Reflection question:** What is the quietest signal my body is sending me right now – and am I willing to listen?

Invitation

You don't need to feel ready.
You just need to be willing.
Willing to notice. To pause. To admit what's been true beneath the pace, the performance, the pushing through.

Listening is not a skill you master. It's a relationship you remember.
A return to what your body has been whispering beneath the noise.

Like Sarah, you may begin with doubt or discomfort. That doesn't disqualify you – it qualifies you. Because resistance doesn't mean it's wrong. It means it matters. It means you're touching something real.

If you've made it here, you've already begun. You've listened – even for a breath, a flicker, a moment. And that moment is enough to begin again.

Listening reveals the signal. But to truly reconnect, you can't stop at hearing.

You must learn to understand.
What is this tension saying?
Why does your gut clench when you stay silent?
Why does your breath shallow the moment responsibility walks in?

In the next chapter we'll explore how to interpret these signals – not as problems to eliminate, but as patterns to decode.
Because your body doesn't speak in noise. It speaks in meaning.
And those meanings hold the truth of what you need, and what must change.

Let's learn how to understand – clearly, gently, and powerfully.

CHAPTER 3

Understand

When symptoms become signals

What does it mean to understand your symptoms?

Listening is the first moment of awareness – the pause where you notice a headache rising, your breath shortening, or a familiar ache returning.

But *understanding* is where your relationship with your body truly begins.

Understanding means you stop treating your symptoms as problems to fix, and start recognising them as *messages to translate*.

It's not just asking 'What's wrong with me?' – it's daring to ask: **'What is my body trying to communicate that I've been too busy, too scared, or too conditioned to hear?'**

This is the moment when healing becomes personal. When you realise your body isn't random or broken – it's intelligent. It's precise.

And it's been speaking the whole time:
- That tension in your shoulders after a conversation you didn't want to have.
- The stomach flutters before you enter a room where you've been dismissed before.

- The fatigue that hits not after exertion, but after self-abandonment.

Your body holds the *story of your life,* not in words, but in patterns.
It remembers where you shrink to stay safe. Where you perform instead of express. Where you override truth to maintain peace.

To understand your symptoms is to learn the language your feelings and experiences speak – a language based not on logic, but on what you live through.

This is not about diagnosing. It's about decoding.

Because when you begin to understand, you're no longer fighting your body.

You're listening to the part of you that never stopped trying to protect you – even when you stopped hearing it.
And that's where everything changes

Why does understanding matter?

Most people don't ignore their symptoms because they don't care – they ignore them because no one ever taught them to listen differently.

So they manage the migraines with medication. They suppress the anxiety with productivity. Or they numb the tension with screens, snacks, or silence. And push past the fatigue with caffeine and willpower.

They treat the symptom like an inconvenience – instead of the insight it really is.

But when you don't understand the message, the body has no choice but to speak louder. What begins as a whisper becomes a warning. A tight chest. A clenched jaw. A deep exhaustion that sleep can't fix.

Understanding is what shifts your lens. It transforms frustration into clarity. It gives your discomfort a purpose – and your experience, a voice.

When you understand, you stop reacting to your body as the problem. You start responding to it as a partner.

This shift doesn't just change how you treat symptoms. It changes how you treat *yourself*.

Because the moment you realise your symptoms aren't setbacks – they're signals – is the moment you stop working against your body, and begin working with it.

When should you decode your symptoms?

Every time a symptom returns, your body is repeating itself – not to annoy you, but to be heard.

It's not random. It's not a weakness.
It's communication.

That 4pm headache that hits like clockwork?
The gut discomfort that flares before Monday's team meeting?
The chest tightness after every phone call with your parent or partner?

These aren't isolated events. They are patterns. And patterns are teachers.
If it shows up more than once, it's not just a symptom.

It's a signal waiting to be decoded.

Your body is telling you where your boundaries are thin. Where your needs are unmet. Where your truth is being silenced.

And the moment you choose to decode that signal – instead of dismissing it – you shift from surviving to understanding.

Where does this understanding happen?

Understanding doesn't arrive in the middle of the chaos. It doesn't appear while you're rushing, reacting, or pushing through.

It arrives in the pause:
- In the quiet after a difficult conversation.
- In the stillness of your car before walking into work.
- In the few minutes before sleep, when your guard finally drops.
- In the space between stimulus and response, when you *choose* to notice.

You don't need an hour.
You need *permission* – to stop, to ask, to feel.

True understanding is found in the moments you usually skip.

And those skipped moments are where you've been waiting to connect with yourself.

How do you start?

Use the **DECODE Map**™ to understand your symptoms. It is not about diagnosis. It's about discovery.
The DECODE Map is a guided path that helps you explore *one* recurring symptom – gently, curiously, and without pressure.
It doesn't just ask, 'What's causing this?' – it invites a deeper question:

'What is my body trying to show me about how I live?'

Because your health is not just physical.
It's relational. It's emotional. It's patterned.

This map helps you connect the dots between how you feel and how you function, so you stop managing symptoms – and start *understanding* them.

It's not complex. But it *is* courageous.

My experience

The DECODE Map didn't begin in the clinic. It began in 2017, in a season of total depletion – when I genuinely believed I was about to die.

I don't say that lightly. I'm a positive person, energetic, and have a high capacity. The kind of person who pushes through, who finds the silver lining, who keeps going.

But that year… I had nothing left in the tank.

I remember lying on the floor one evening, my body aching and my mind fogged, thinking: 'That's it. I'm done. This is the end of me.'

And then, barely a whisper – a voice I can still feel today, I heard: **'Don't give up now. You can do this.'**

That was the moment something shifted. Not dramatically. Not instantly. But enough.

I began listening. Not out of wisdom, but out of survival, because I could no longer outrun my symptoms.

During those first few weeks of recovery I wasn't trying to create a system. I was trying to stay upright, trying to understand what my body had been saying all along.

I started paying attention – really paying attention – to the symptoms that had followed me for years:

- The fatigue that no amount of sleep resolved.
- The stomach pain that flared in moments of stress.
- The shortness of breath that came not from effort, but from self-abandonment.

And what I found wasn't just discomfort. It was grief. Grief for all the times I overrode my body's truth. Grief for how little I had been taught – at school, at home, even in my professional training – about how to *feel*, not just function.

That was when the **DECODE Map** began to form. Not in theory, but in tenderness.
Each insight came with both sadness and clarity.
Each symptom carried not just pain, but *pattern*.

And as I followed those patterns, I stopped treating my symptoms as puzzles to solve. I started seeing them as messages to respect.

That's when everything changed. Not quickly. Not perfectly. But *truthfully*.

The DECODE Map was born in that space – between surrender and self-respect.

Between collapse and clarity.

And it's now helped hundreds of clients move from confusion to comprehension – not because they worked harder, but because they finally understood:

Their body wasn't malfunctioning. It was speaking.

The DECODE Map

Use this simple guide to explore the story behind your symptoms:

D – Describe the sensation	What does it feel like? Sharp, heavy, numb?
E – Examine the timing	When does it show – time of day, after certain activities?
C – Consider the context	What's happening around you when it appears?
O – Observe the pattern	Is it linked to certain people, thoughts, or places?
D – Determine the need	What might your body be asking for – rest, boundaries, expression?
E – Explore the emotion	What feelings surface when you notice this symptom?

Apply this to one recurring symptom, and you'll begin to see connections you couldn't see before.

Even though these steps are straightforward, applying them is an act of courage, because once you understand your body's language, you can no longer pretend not to know.

Let's dive deeper.

D – Describe the sensation

What are you actually feeling – physically – in your body, right now?

This isn't about fixing, analysing, or diagnosing. It's about noticing what's *real*, without needing to change it.

Ask yourself:
- Is it tight or heavy?
- Is it sharp, dull, warm, or numb?
- Is it buzzing, pulsing, clenched, or stuck?

If putting words to it feels difficult, try speaking it like you would to a friend:
- 'It feels like a knot in my stomach.'
- 'It's like a weight is pressing on my chest.'
- 'It's like I've been holding my breath without realising it.'

Still unsure?

Place your hand gently on the area. Close your eyes. Say: 'I notice…' – and finish the sentence with whatever comes.

You can't get it wrong.

This step is not about control. It's about contact.

It's about bringing language to sensation – because the moment you can describe something, you're no longer lost in it.

You've created space.

Why this matters

Most people skip this step. They jump straight to: 'How do I stop this?' But if you don't know what it is, how can you respond to it with care? Describing the sensation is how you start a relationship with your body's signals.

Not to judge them. Not to suppress them. But simply to meet what's there – honestly, kindly, and without rush.

This is the first act of understanding.

E – Examine the timing

When does this sensation usually show?
Understanding the *when* is often the key to unlocking the *why*.

Ask yourself:
- What time of day does it appear – morning, mid-afternoon, late at night?
- Does it flare up before or after certain events – meetings, meals, conversations?
- Is it tied to the start of your week? The end of your day?
- Does it always follow a specific kind of interaction or thought?

You're not just tracking symptoms. You're tracking rhythms – your body's internal clock and emotional map.

Why this matters

Timing holds truth.

Recurring pain at 4pm might not be about posture – it could be about the emotional weight of the day.

Waking at 3am with anxiety might not be random – it could be the only time your body has your attention.

This is where many people overlook their body's intelligence.

They dismiss repeated timing as coincidence, rather than communication.

Try this

Keep a simple log for three days. Each time the sensation appears, note:
- the time
- what just happened
- what you were thinking or feeling.

You'll begin to see patterns you've never realised.

This step is about recognising that your body doesn't just react randomly. It reacts *on time* – to pressure, to silence, to unspoken truths.

The timing is not the problem. It's the breadcrumb trail.

C – Consider the context

What's happening around you when the symptom appears?

Context reveals what content alone can't.
It's not just *what* you feel, but *where* you are, *who* you're with, and *what* is unfolding when the symptom arrives.

Ask yourself:
- Where am I when this happens – home, work, driving, in a meeting?
- Who am I with – or whom did I just interact with?
- What was I doing or thinking just before the sensation began?
- What story or expectation was I carrying in that moment?

You're looking for emotional proximity, not just physical location.

Sometimes the tightness in your chest shows, *not* because of what was said, but because of what *wasn't*.

Why this matters

Your body reacts to context long before your mind makes sense of it.
Pain in your stomach after an email from your boss isn't about digestion – it's about hierarchy, pressure, or unresolved tension.

This step is about widening the lens.
Symptoms don't live in isolation. They live in scenes. And those scenes carry emotional fingerprints – beliefs, roles, histories, expectations.

Try this

The next time a familiar discomfort appears, pause and ask yourself:
- What's happening right now – not just around me, but inside me?
- Is this a pattern of being needed, dismissed, overruled, or overlooked?

Write it down – even in bullet points. You'll begin to see that your body's messages are embedded in moments, not just muscles.

This step builds the bridge between physical sensation and emotional landscape.

Once you see the scene, you can begin to rewrite the script.

O – Observe the pattern

Is the symptom linked to certain people, thoughts, or environments?

This is where the dots begin to connect.

Ask yourself:
- When does this symptom *usually* show? Before deadlines, after family visits, on Sunday evenings?
- Is there a repeat character in this story? A person, situation, or topic that reliably triggers it?
- What thoughts or beliefs tend to accompany this feeling? 'I have to get this right.' 'They'll be disappointed.' 'I'm falling behind.'

Look for:
- Recurring times of day or week.
- Repeated environments (the car, your office, your childhood home).
- Emotional loops (shame, resentment, fear of failure).

Why this matters

Patterns are protection in disguise.
Your body isn't reacting randomly. It's responding consistently to what it perceives as unsafe, overwhelming, or misaligned.
But you can't change what you don't see.
Pattern recognition is what gives you the power to choose something different.

Try this

Complete the sentence:
'This symptom often appears when I...'

Example answers:
- '...agree to something I don't want to do.'
- '...get asked for help but I'm already exhausted.'
- '...anticipate being judged.'

Patterns may start with pain – but they end in clarity.
Once you see the pattern, you're no longer trapped in it.
You're in relationship with it. And that's where transformation begins.

D – Determine the need

What might your body be asking for?

Every symptom is a signal – not just of what hurts, but of what's missing.

Ask yourself:
- If this part of my body had a voice, what would it ask for?
- What does this sensation need right now – not to go away, but to feel supported?

Possible needs:
- **Rest** – not because you're lazy, but because you're human.
- **Boundaries** – to protect your energy, time, or truth.
- **Expression** – to let out what you've been holding in.
- **Reassurance** – a reminder that you're safe, not failing.
- **Space** – to breathe, think, or feel without rushing.

Why this matters

You can't meet a need you can't name.
And when needs go unmet, symptoms amplify until you're forced to listen.

Most people ask, 'How do I get rid of this feeling?'
A better question is: 'What is this feeling trying to get me to notice?'

Try this

Complete the sentence: 'What I need right now is…'

Example answers:
- '…five minutes of silence.'
- '…permission to not fix everything.'
- '…to say no without guilt.'

Your body is not asking for perfection.
It's asking for presence.
Meeting your needs – even in small ways – is how you rebuild trust with your body.

E – Explore the emotion

What feelings come up when you notice this symptom?

Beneath every physical sensation is an emotional thread.
This doesn't mean your pain is 'just emotional'.

It means that your body and emotions speak the same language – you just haven't been taught to translate it.

Ask yourself:
- What emotion is riding alongside this sensation? Is it sadness? Resentment? Fear? Disappointment?
- Is this a familiar feeling – one that shows up in other parts of your life?
- What might I be feeling that I haven't had space to name?

Still unsure?

Use simple language:
- 'This feels like a weight of sadness.'
- 'It's like my body is bracing for something.'
- 'It reminds me of the last time I felt dismissed.'

Why this matters

When you ignore the emotion, the body has to scream louder.
When you meet it, even quietly, the body softens.

This step isn't about fixing the feeling – it's about facing it.
Most people never get this far. They stop in pain and try to push through.
But if you sit with the emotion – not to dramatise it, but to honour it – you reclaim your internal clarity.

Try this

Complete the sentence:
'When I feel this sensation, the emotion underneath is…'

Example answers:

- '...grief for what I've ignored.'
- '... anger about being unseen.'
- '... fear of what slowing down might reveal.'

Remember:
- Naming an emotion doesn't mean you have to act on it.
- It means you've stopped pretending it's not there.
- And that is one of the most powerful steps towards reconnection.

Real stories – understanding in action

These are not case studies. They're lived experiences.

They are moments when the body spoke louder than the mind – and someone finally listened deeply enough to translate.

In each story you'll see how understanding symptoms wasn't about analysis or control. It was about context, compassion, and courage.

Let these stories remind you: what you feel is not random. It's remembered. And it can be understood.

Rebuilding self-trust from the inside out

Jessy, 24, was a bright, creative woman who had just stepped into the workforce. On the surface she appeared capable and focused – but under the surface she was emotionally untethered. After being unexpectedly laid off from her first job in social media, her confidence collapsed.

For seven months Jessy couldn't secure a job – not even warehouse packing work. 'It felt like I was failing at life,' she later told me. Her mind raced with self-doubt. Her body shut down in interviews. She stopped sleeping. She lived with a quiet heaviness that wouldn't lift.

By the time she started the OsteoLife LUCKY System, she was running on hope – not belief.

She described herself as feeling 'disconnected', low on energy, and emotionally saturated. She was going through the motions without any sense of presence. Her body felt like a burden, not a guide.

Slowly things shifted.

In one guided pause she noticed a tightness in her chest – something she'd previously ignored. As she stayed with it, emotion surfaced.

She said, 'I hadn't realised how much I was storing and suppressing.'

That moment broke open a new awareness.

Jessy began noticing how she abandoned herself in interviews – bracing for rejection, contorting to fit what she thought others wanted.

She started checking in before big decisions. Was this aligned – or automatic? Was she showing up with clarity – or performing out of fear?

Then her entire energy shifted. She felt calmer, more grounded. More loving with herself. Others noticed too. 'You seem lighter,' one friend said.

Three weeks later she landed a job – and the hiring manager commented, 'You came across so clear and confident.'

Now Jessy doesn't push through. She pauses. She checks in. She listens.

That pause is now her power.

'I've learnt to slow down and check in with my body instead of always powering through from my head. That shift has helped me make clearer, more aligned decisions and feel more stable in my everyday life.'

What changed for Jessy?

- She stopped seeing anxiety as a flaw and began treating it as a message.
- She learnt to pause before interviews and decisions, checking for alignment.
- She rebuilt her self-trust from the inside out.

Lessons learnt

- Suppressed emotions don't go away – they wait for you to listen.
- Presence begins with noticing what's real, not what's expected.
- Confidence isn't pushed – it's grounded.

How is Jessy now?

Jessy has transformed from disconnected and overwhelmed to grounded and self-trusting through the OsteoLife LUCKY System. She learned to treat anxiety not as a flaw, but as a valuable message, using conscious pauses to check alignment before interviews and important decisions.

This shifted her energy, boosting clarity and calm, which others noticed as newfound confidence. Her pause is now a source of intelligence and presence, helping her choose not just any job, but one that feels truly aligned.

When understanding becomes liberation

Malik, 42, was a consultant with a reputation for excellence. His clients trust him. His colleagues respect him. And his family admire how hard he works to build the life they shared.

But behind the polished surface, Malik was running only on fumes.

When he first sat across from me, he looked exhausted in a way that went beyond lack of sleep. His skin was pale, and his eyes were clouded with a fatigue that didn't lift even when he tried to smile.

He listed his symptoms in a flat, practiced tone, as though reading from someone else's chart:
- Chronic gut issues that flared unpredictably.
- Restless nights filled with racing thoughts.
- A short temper that was starting to spill into his marriage and work.

'I just assumed it was part of being successful,' he admitted, rubbing a hand over his face. 'Everyone I know feels like this.'

But as he spoke it became clear he no longer believed that that was a good enough reason. He was tired of feeling like his body was about to betray him.

When I introduced the DECODE Map, Malik listened carefully, nodding along – though I could see the scepticism in his jaw.

'So… you're saying that my symptoms are trying to tell me something?' he asked, a quiet edge of disbelief in his voice.

'Yes,' I told him. 'They're not here to punish you. They're here to guide you.'

He agreed to start small. One symptom. One week. He chose his unpredictable stomach pain.

At first the process felt mechanical. He would jot down the sensation, log the time it appeared, then list what was happening around him.

But then something clicked.

One afternoon, after delivering a high-stakes pitch, Malik felt the familiar ache in his gut. This time, instead of brushing it off or blaming lunch, he paused.

He realised the pain wasn't about what he ate. It was about what he had swallowed:
- His instincts.
- His discomfort.
- His need to say no.

He described it as a moment of quiet clarity. A single thread tugging at years of compliance.

'My body isn't broken,' he said. 'It's the only part of me that's been honest.'

From that moment Malik began making subtle but deliberate changes.

He restructured his week to protect his energy. He stopped saying yes to projects out of obligation. He started journaling after client calls – releasing the tension he used to suppress.

Within weeks his gut issues softened. Not because of a new diet. And not because of medication.

But because he finally stopped ignoring what his body had been asking for.

His wife noticed first. One evening, she looked across the dinner table and said, 'You're different. You feel lighter. More… here.'

Months later Malik still uses the DECODE Map. He doesn't see discomfort as a setback. He treats it as insight – an invitation to align.

When I asked what changed, he said: '**I stopped treating my body like an obstacle. I started treating it like a partner.**'

What changed for Malik?

- He began to trust that his symptoms were communication, not failure.
- He stopped sacrificing himself for success.
- He realised that slowing down could be a strategy – not a setback.

Lessons learnt

- Ignoring discomfort never makes it go away – it only makes it louder.
- Understanding your body requires curiosity, not judgement.
- Real change starts with listening to the truth you'd rather avoid.

How is Malik now?

Malik has shifted from running on fumes to partnering with his body's signals. Using the DECODE Map, he learned to treat symptoms not as failures but as meaningful communication.

This has brought deliberate changes: protecting energy, saying no to obligations, and processing tension instead of suppressing it.

He no longer sacrifices himself for success, and embraces slowing down as a strategic choice. His presence and alignment now guide how he shows up both at work and home.

When the body remembers before you do

Tom, 27, was a dedicated athlete who trained with an intensity that left little room for anything else. He was preparing for his first major running competition – a goal he'd been chasing for years.

From the outside he looked like the picture of health: lean, focused, and disciplined. But by the time he came to see me, that confidence had cracked. And underneath it, something deeper was unravelling.

A few weeks before race day, Tom had started experiencing sudden, overwhelming episodes of breathlessness. He'd begin his warm-up feeling fine. Then his chest would go tight. He got shallow breath. And panic set in, as if the air had been sucked out of the room.

The first time it happened, he froze. His heart raced, and his vision blurred. He was convinced he was having a medical emergency.

He saw specialists – cardiologists, pulmonologists, and neurologists. Every test came back clean. 'There's nothing wrong,' they said. 'Maybe it's stress.'

But Tom didn't feel stressed. He felt betrayed. By his own body. By the silence of every scan that couldn't explain what he was living through.

When he finally walked into my clinic, he didn't speak the language of vulnerability. He wore stoicism like armour.

'I feel ridiculous,' he muttered. 'I'm supposed to be strong. And now I can't even trust my own breath.'

At first his body was braced – tense, protective, and fighting itself.

We started simple: hands-on work to release the diaphragm, ribs, and back. Movement began to return where it had been tight.

Then I taught him a breathing rhythm – a short practice to anchor his body when the wave of panic hit. It wasn't a quick fix. But it was a crack in the wall. The beginning of trust.

Over time he softened. He trained again. And months later he stood at the starting line – present, calm, and connected.

A year passed. And he returned.

This time it wasn't a crisis. It was a quiet whisper. His breath was tight again – not like before, but familiar enough to make him nervous.

He had a new relationship, and his career was expanding. But beneath it all his body had remembered.

We didn't start with breathing techniques. We started with the OsteoLife LUCKY System.

He closed his eyes and listened. There it was, a steady ache of fear deep beneath his ribs – the burden of his own expectations. The voice inside told him, 'You're only strong when you stay silent.' But this time, he faced it instead of running.

He traced the signals. He honoured the memory.

He understood that his body wasn't breaking down. It was speaking up.

By the end of our session his shoulders had dropped, and his chest felt open. His face was clear.

'I think... I finally appreciate my body,' he said. 'I get what it's been trying to protect me from.'

He left that day, not trying to fix himself, but to be a partner to himself.

What changed for Tom?

- He stopped treating anxiety as an enemy to conquer.
- He realised that listening to his body was not weakness – it was strength.
- He reclaimed trust – in his breath, his body, and his story.

Lessons learnt

- Even the strongest bodies can carry unspoken fear.
- Real resilience is built on connection, not control.
- Respecting your body's signals can transform how you show up when it matters most.

How is Tom now?

Tom has transformed his relationship with anxiety and his body. He no longer fights breathlessness as an enemy, but listens deeply to what his body communicates.

Through the OsteoLife LUCKY System and breathwork, he reclaimed trust in his breath and self, shifting from stoic control to embodied partnership. Now, he trains intensely but with presence and respect — not fear. Breathing through pressure rather than running from it.

Try this today – the daily DECODE

Understanding begins not with control, but with curiosity.
Today, choose one recurring symptom – tight shoulders, a clenched jaw, restless sleep, gut discomfort – anything your body has been whispering (or shouting) repeatedly.
Don't try to fix it. Just walk it through the **DECODE Map**, one step at a time.

D – Describe the sensation

What are you *actually* feeling in your body – right now?
Is it sharp, heavy, dull, numb?
Buzzing, clenched, stuck, tight?
Say it out loud or write it down.

'It feels like a knot in my chest.'
'Like a slow pressure behind my eyes.'
'Like I'm holding my breath and didn't realise it.'
Give it language. Not to solve it. Just to meet it.

E – Examine the timing

When does it tend to show?
Is it always after lunch? Late at night? Before meetings? After phone calls?
Timing is never random. It is a rhythm revealing itself.

C – Consider the context

What's happening around you when the sensation appears?

Where are you? Who are you with? What just happened – or what are you anticipating?

O – Observe the pattern

Does this symptom repeat under similar circumstances?
Begin to link the dots between the external moment and the internal signal. Patterns are messages waiting to be heard.

D – Determine the need

What might your body be asking for?
Is it rest? Boundaries? Expression? Solitude? A walk? A pause?
Ask gently: 'What do you need from me right now?'

E – Explore the emotion

Beneath the sensation, what feeling lives there?
Is it sadness? Resentment? Fear? Loneliness?

Let the feeling rise without judgement. This is how truth surfaces.

Optional practice

- **Notebook check-in:** Keep a small notebook nearby. Each day, write one sentence describing what you noticed in your body. No pressure. Just pattern-tracking with compassion.

- **Evening reflection:** Before bed, close your eyes and ask, 'What did my body try to show me today?' Write down one insight, no matter how small.

- **Name it aloud:** If you feel stuck, place your hand on the area of discomfort and whisper, 'I notice...' Let whatever comes to mind finish the sentence.

Why this matters

Most people run from their symptoms, trying to silence them.
But when you stay, when you listen, and when you name without fixing, you shift the entire relationship.
This is where understanding begins.

Not in logic, but in presence.
Let today be the first day your symptom becomes a signal.
Not something you push through, but something you *partner with*.

Pause and reflect – a moment with your body

Before you turn the page, take a quiet breath.

Let your shoulders soften. Let your attention drop from your mind into your body. Not to analyse, but to be present.

Now, ask yourself:

1 – What symptom has been tapping you on the shoulder – repeatedly – but you've learnt to ignore, dismiss, or explain it away?
Maybe it's that familiar tightness in your chest, the afternoon headache, the Sunday-night stomach ache.
What have you come to accept as 'just the way it is'?

2 – If that symptom could speak, what might it be trying to say?
Not in judgement. Not in blame. Just... a message.

Is it saying, 'Slow down'?
Or, 'Please stop saying yes when you mean no?'
Or, 'This isn't aligned with who you are anymore?'

3 – What is your default response when discomfort shows up?
Do you override it? Numb it?
Do you try to 'fix' it as quickly as possible so it doesn't disrupt your day?
What does that pattern cost you over time?

4 – What would it feel like to stay, just for a moment, with the discomfort – not to change it, but to hear it?
Could you offer your body the same curiosity you would offer a friend in pain?

5 – What's one small, doable step you can take this week to understand your body more clearly?
Not a transformation. Not a routine overhaul.
Just one act of attention that says, 'I'm here. I'm listening.'

These questions are not a test. They are an invitation.

You don't need to answer them perfectly. You only need to answer honestly. This is how self-respect begins – by letting your body have a voice.

When you're ready, we'll explore how to connect those signals to the way you live, relate, and lead.

DECODE Map worksheet

Refer to the OsteoLife LUCKY Toolkit at the back of this book for the DECODE Map worksheet. Use it as guided space to track one recurring symptom with presence, clarity, and compassion.

This is where understanding becomes a practice, not just a concept.

It's how you begin to connect dots that once felt random... and reclaim meaning from what your body has been trying to tell you all along.

Chapter 3 tool recap

- **DECODE Map** – Apply it to one recurring symptom – gently, consistently, with curiosity.
- **Daily DECODE practice** – Notice. Reflect. Record. One signal at a time.
- **Reflection question:** What pattern keeps repeating – and what might it be asking me to finally see?

When you bring intention to what your body repeats, you stop reacting and start relating.
That's not management – that's partnership.
And that's where change begins.

Invitation

If understanding feels overwhelming or unfamiliar, pause here.
Your body is not asking you to solve everything.
It's asking you to stay in the conversation.

You don't need perfect clarity.
You need willingness. A softening. The courage to stay curious, even when the answers aren't immediate.

Because, now you've begun to see the difference between suppression and understanding. Between symptoms and signals.
And this is where the shift deepens.

In the next chapter, you'll learn how to move from insight to intimacy – how to connect the dots between what you feel, how you live, and what your body has always known.

This isn't about fixing.

It's about belonging to yourself in a way you may have never been taught, but have always deserved.

Let's take the next step – connecting.

CHAPTER 4

Connecting

> *Connect the dots between your patterns, your choices,*
> *and your physical cues.*

What does it mean to connect with your body?

Listening means noticing what your body is telling you. For example, if your stomach hurts, that is a signal.

Understanding means learning what that signal means. Like, maybe your stomach hurts because you are hungry or nervous. Understanding is learning the language.

But connecting is the most important part. This is where it all makes sense.

Connecting means seeing the whole story your body is telling.

It's not just about the pain or feeling you have. It's about understanding how that pain relates to your daily life. For example, maybe the stomach pain comes when you are stressed about work or worried about family.

Connecting helps you see how your feelings, habits, and body signals all come together.

That 4pm headache? It's not just about posture or screen time. It might be the cost of bracing yourself through hours of conversations where you couldn't speak your truth.

That tightness in your stomach after lunch? It's not just indigestion. It might be the tension you've been swallowing with every polite 'I'm fine'.

That low-grade fatigue that never lifts? It's not just about sleep. It could be the silent weight of performing, producing, and pretending every single day.

No symptom lives in isolation.

Your body isn't fragmented, even if the world has taught you to treat it that way. Each ache, each wave of tiredness, each pang of tension is a dot.

And those dots form a map.

A map of how you've been surviving. A map of what you've been carrying. A map of where disconnection took root – and where reconnection wants to begin.

This isn't about blaming yourself for the pain. It's about honouring it with the one thing it's been asking for all along: your attention.

Because, until you see the full picture, you can't shift the pattern. And you can't change what you refuse to see.

Connection is clarity. And clarity is the first step towards choice.

Why does connecting matter?

You can know you're exhausted… and still not know *why*.
You can track your sleep, your steps, or your meals… and still feel stuck.

You can say, 'I'm anxious', or 'I'm tense', or 'I'm wired'… and still not understand what's fuelling it beneath the surface.

That's because awareness on its own isn't enough.

True change begins when you connect the dots.

Change begins when you start tracing the invisible threads between your choices and your symptoms – what you say yes to, what you suppress, how you move through the world – and how your body responds.

Connection is what turns vague discomfort into meaningful direction.

It's what transforms overwhelm into insight.

It's the shift from 'Why is this happening to me?' to 'What is this trying to show me?'

When you connect the dots, you stop seeing your body as unreliable or dramatic. And you start seeing it as intelligent: communicating, not complaining. Not punishing, but pointing.

Your symptoms aren't random. They are your body's way of getting your attention.

And once you see the pattern, you're no longer trapped in reaction. You have the power to choose differently.

This is how self-respect begins: not with perfection, but with perspective.

When should you connect?

Connect anytime you feel stuck or frustrated, especially when you start to give up.
Connect when your body keeps sending the same signals, but you stop asking why.
Pay attention to thoughts like:
'I don't know why this keeps happening.'
'This is just how I am.'
'I guess this is my normal.'

These are not facts. They are clues that you've lost touch with what your body is really trying to tell you.

You are not random.
Your tiredness, tight muscles, and aches are part of a pattern. And every pattern has a story.
When your busy life hides what your body needs you to hear, pause.
Don't try harder – look back.
Look back at your choices, your stress, and the places and people that affect you.

Connecting is how you take back control.
Not by doing more – but by understanding what's already inside you.

Where should you connect?

Connection doesn't require a whole retreat. It just requires your attention. Mapping happens in small, honest moments – moments you already have, if you're willing to use them, such as:

- at the end of the day, when your body feels heavier than it should
- in the silence after a meeting that left you depleted
- in the pause before you reach for your phone to numb out
- in that breath between reacting and reflecting.

This isn't about carving out more time. It's about reclaiming the time you already spend ignoring what matters.

Because clarity doesn't come from controlling more – it comes from observing differently.

You don't need hours. You need honesty. And the willingness to stop, to notice, and to write down what your body has been carrying all along.

That's where patterns emerge.

And that's where the real map begins.

How do you start?

You no longer have to guess about what to do.

The **CONTEXT Map**™ is a practical, compassionate tool to help you see what's really shaping your body's responses. Not just what you felt, but what surrounded it. Not just the symptom, but the system it lives in.

The CONTEXT Map gives structure to something that often feels overwhelming:
- Why you keep feeling drained after meetings.
- Why your gut flares at the same time every week.
- Why sleep feels elusive even when you're exhausted.

It's not a diagnostic tool. It's a clarity tool. Because when you're in a fog, the most powerful thing you can do is trace the pattern by looking at:
- What your choices were that day.

- What pressure you were under.
- Where you were. Who you were with.
- What expectations were pulling at you.

This is how confusion becomes clarity, and self-blame becomes self-leadership.
The CONTEXT Map isn't about finding fault. It's about finding alignment.
You don't need to overhaul your life in one go.
You need a place to begin seeing clearly – and this is it.

My experience

For years, I thought my symptoms were separate from my choices.

When I felt exhausted, I blamed my schedule. When my stomach tightened, I blamed the food. When I snapped at someone I loved, I blamed hormones.

I never stopped to ask how it all connected. I didn't see a pattern – I only saw problems.

Then came mid-June 2017 – a time I'll never forget.

That morning, I collapsed. I couldn't move or think. Fear washed over me. I called an ambulance, sure something was wrong with my body.

The paramedics checked my blood pressure, oxygen, and heart rate. Everything was normal. On the outside I was falling apart, but inside, my body was still holding on.

In that quiet moment, eyes closed and tears welling, I whispered 'Thank you' to my body. Not just from relief, but out of respect.

Thank you for still working when I didn't. Thank you for warning me. Thank you for not giving up, even when I ignored you.

That was when I began to truly connect.

I stopped treating my body as a problem to fix and started seeing it as a partner. I placed my hand over my chest, and promised, 'I will not abandon you again.'

From then on, I noticed patterns I had never seen before.

I remember one week vividly. I had been powering through – back-to-back clients, admin at night, early workouts I didn't have the energy for.

On paper, I was doing everything right: daily movement, balanced meals and meditation.

But underneath, my life felt like a checklist of compliance – not connection. Besides journaling what I was grateful for each day, I also wrote about how those moments made me feel, what I learned from them, and, most importantly, how my body responded. This helped me build a deeper connection with myself.

Beyond simply journaling what I was grateful for each day, I traced:
- every rushed meal I ate standing up
- every 'yes' I gave when I had nothing left to give
- every boundary I violated to be liked, to be useful
- every time I ignored my gut to stay in control.

What emerged wasn't chaos. It was a pattern – a map revealing how disconnected I'd become. Writing these details alongside how they made me feel, what I learned, and how my body responded, helped me move from mere compliance to deeper connection with myself.

My fatigue wasn't about overwork. It was about over-giving.

My gut pain wasn't about food. It was about the truth I kept swallowing.

My irritability wasn't about hormones. It was about the self-abandonment I kept normalising.

That's when the **CONTEXT Map** was born. Not as a theory, but as survival. As a lifeline. Once I saw the connections, I could no longer pretend not to know.

When you start tracing how your choices, obligations, and environments shape your symptoms, you stop feeling like a victim of your body – and start leading from within it.

You stop seeing pain as punishment and start treating it as a prompt: '**Pay attention. This matters.**'

And everything changes from there.

The CONTEXT Map

Use this simple guide to trace the hidden relationships between your body's signals and your daily life:

C – Choices	What decisions are shaping how your body feels?
O – Obligations	What roles, expectations, or unspoken rules influence your behaviour?
N – Nutrition	How are you fuelling your body, and how does it affect your state?
T – Time use	How did you spend your time, and did that reflect your values or survival mode?
E – Environment	What spaces are you in, and how do they shape your nervous system?
X – External Stressors	What unseen pressures or tensions are quietly weighing on you?
T – Triggers	What moments or thoughts activate a physical response?

Apply this to one recurring symptom – and you'll begin to see how your experience is connected, not random.

Let's dive deeper.

C – Choices

What decisions are shaping how your body feels?

These can be obvious (what you eat, how much you work), or subtle (what you tolerate, what you avoid).

Ask yourself:
- What did I say yes to that I didn't want to?
- What did I ignore, suppress, or push through?
- Were my actions aligned with my energy or against it?

This step is about tracing how your moment-to-moment decisions shape your internal experience.

O – Obligations

What roles, expectations, or unspoken rules are influencing your behaviour?

Obligations can be external (deadlines, family duties) or internal (perfectionism, people-pleasing).

Ask yourself:
- What pressures did I feel today?
- Who or what am I trying not to disappoint?
- Where did I override my truth to meet someone else's?

Most people don't realise how much their nervous system is shaped by unacknowledged pressure. Here's where you name it.

N – Nutrition

How are you fuelling your body – and how does that impact your state?
This isn't about judgement. It's about observation.

Ask yourself:
- Did I eat regularly or skip meals?
- Did I eat with presence, or while distracted and rushed?
- Did I notice any reactions after eating – tiredness, bloating, tension?

Food is a rhythm, not just a resource. It reflects how you care for yourself under pressure.

T – Time use

How did you spend your time – and did it reflect your values or your survival mode?

Ask yourself:
- Where did my energy go today?
- Did I have space to rest, or was it all output?
- Did I lose time in habits that don't nourish me (scrolling, overworking, avoidance)?

Time is your most honest mirror. This step shows you what you're prioritising – and what it's costing.

E – Environment

What spaces are you spending time in, and how do they shape your nervous system?

Ask yourself:
- Was I in calm or chaotic spaces?
- Were there loud noises, clutter, conflict, or too much stimulation?
- Was I somewhere that made me feel small, rushed, or unseen?

Environments speak to your body long before your mind registers discomfort. This is where you learn to name that impact.

X – External Stressors

What external events or dynamics are weighing on you – consciously or not?

This includes the news, financial stress, family conflict, uncertainty, or even collective tension.

Ask yourself:
- What's been quietly draining me in the background?
- What's unresolved that I keep pushing to the side?
- What am I carrying that isn't entirely mine?

This is where you locate the unseen weight – so it doesn't shape your body in silence.

T – Triggers

What moments, interactions, or thoughts activated a physical response?

Ask yourself:
- When did I feel activated or shut down today?
- What set off the tension, fatigue, or pain?
- What story did my body believe in that moment?

This final step helps you trace the emotional fingerprint behind your physical signals. It gives you clarity, not control.

Apply the CONTEXT Map to one recurring symptom – and you'll stop asking: 'Why is this happening?' Instead, you'll begin to see how it is connected.

These steps are simple, but not always easy. They require honesty, presence, and the willingness to listen when silence feels safer.

But if you can stay curious, the CONTEXT Map will return something deeper than relief: clarity, authority, and the ability to make different choices.

You are not at the mercy of your symptoms. You are in a relationship with them.

This map helps you lead that relationship – deliberately, consistently, and with compassion.

Real stories – connecting in action

These stories are not just anecdotes – they are *lived experiences* that reveal how deeply the body holds the truth beyond the mind's chatter. They show what happens when someone listens with compassion and courage, moving past judgement to embrace context and feeling.

Witness these journeys of reclaiming self-trust from the inside out. These moments remind us that our sensations and symptoms are never random; they are memories our body carries and signals we can learn from to heal and transform.

When excellence becomes exhaustion

Veronica was 17 when she first came to see me. Bright, driven, and thriving at her selective high school, she appeared to have everything under control.

She trained competitively in four sports, maintained top marks, and her teachers relied on her. Her parents described her as 'low maintenance'. Her friends called her 'the strong one'.

But beneath the surface, Veronica was unravelling. She hadn't had her period in six months, she woke up nauseous most mornings, and she couldn't sleep through the night. Her body had been sending signals for months – but no one had asked what they meant. Not even her.

'I just feel like I can't stop,' she whispered during our first session. 'If I stop, everything will fall apart.'

In the beginning, the idea of connecting with her body felt uncomfortable. She had learnt to equate rest with failure, listening with weakness, and slowing down with falling behind.

But as we walked through the OsteoLife LUCKY System, something shifted. She began to connect the dots.

The nausea wasn't random. It showed up every time she was around a particular group of friends.

The headaches spiked after long days when she forced herself to smile through discomfort.

The exhaustion deepened when she pushed through, pretending she was fine.

She started to make different choices: she dropped two of her four sports, she distanced herself from the people who drained her, and she let go of the need to be perfect all the time.

And, slowly, her symptoms softened. Not because she found a new strategy – but because she finally stopped abandoning herself.

Then came the real test. She enrolled in university as a psychology major, following the path everyone assumed she would take. But within weeks, her symptoms surged back.

One morning, sitting on a park bench between classes, she placed a hand on her chest and asked, 'What's here?'

This time, the answer was different: 'I want to study engineering.'

It didn't fit the narrative others had for her. But it was true. And this time she didn't override it.

She changed her degree, and two years later she still calls it the most honest decision she's ever made.

What changed for Veronica?

- She stopped measuring her worth by how much she could endure.
- She trusted her symptoms as truth, not weakness.
- She made decisions based on internal alignment, not external approval.

Lessons learnt

- Chronic disconnection can hide behind a polished performance.
- Your body doesn't lie – even when your mind tries to explain it away.

- Real alignment is not about doing less. It's about choosing what's *true*.

How is Veronica now?

Veronica has moved from relentless endurance to aligned authenticity. She learned to trust her body's signals as essential truths rather than weaknesses, leading her to shift from externally driven expectations (a psychology major) to a path that truly fits her (engineering).

Now she pushes forward deliberately, working hard only on what feels right internally, and this has restored her energy and stabilised her symptoms. She no longer waits for physical crashes to listen – her body is her trusted protector, not an enemy.

From resignation to redesign

Paul, 55, was a seasoned architect with decades of experience and success behind him. He had the professional respect of his industry – but also chronic back pain, shoulder stiffness, and jaw tension that no therapy seemed to relieve.

'I think this is just how it is now,' he told me. 'Maybe my body's just… done.'
When I introduced the CONTEXT Map, he was sceptical. But he agreed to try.

Within a week he began to see patterns he had never noticed in 30 years:
- The pain was worst on days he worked over 10 hours without breaks.
- His old desk and chair hadn't changed since his twenties.

- He tensed every time he got a message from one particularly demanding client.

'I thought my back was just getting old,' he said. 'But I think it was trying to get my attention.'

He made small, sustainable changes:
- He included movement breaks in his workday calendar.
- He adjusted his workstation.
- He took actual lunch breaks.

Three months later, he sat across from me and said: 'For the first time in years, I feel like I'm not at war with myself.'

What changed for Paul

- He stopped believing pain was inevitable.
- He took responsibility for the patterns in his environment.
- He reclaimed agency over how he lived and worked.

Lessons learnt

- Symptoms don't always mean decline – they're invitations.
- You can't heal what you don't take the time to observe.
- Sustainable change begins with conscious patterns.

How is Paul now?

Paul has made a remarkable shift from accepting chronic pain as inevitable to actively noticing and changing the patterns fuelling it.

By thoughtfully adjusting his environment, incorporating movement breaks, and honouring real rest, he no longer fights with his body but collaborates with it.

His full-time work now balances presence and intention, not relentless pace or self-sacrifice. Paul has reclaimed agency over his daily rhythm, showing that even decades-old symptoms can improve through conscious, sustainable change.

Try this today – the daily CONTEXT check

This week, choose one recurring symptom – fatigue, tension, pain, or unease – and trace its deeper roots using the CONTEXT Map.

This isn't about blame – it's about gently uncovering the patterns your body already knows.

Give yourself 10 quiet minutes. Let curiosity lead.

C – Choices

What decisions shaped your day?

Did you say yes when you meant no? Did you push through when you needed rest?

O – Obligations

What expectations – internal or external – were weighing on you?
Were you trying to meet a deadline, prove yourself, or avoid disappointing someone?

N – Nutrition

What did nourishment look like?
Did you eat with presence or on autopilot? Did your meals energise you or deplete you?

T – Time use

How did you spend your hours?
Was there space to breathe, or did you move from task to task without pause?

E – Environment

Where were you – physically and emotionally?
Was the space noisy, calm, cluttered, expansive? Who were you with?

X – External stressors

What was happening around you that you had no control over?
News, family conflict, unexpected demands?

T – Triggers

What was the moment it all tipped?
A word, a glance, a message, a memory – what reopened the tension?

Optional practice

- Choose one letter to journal on each day this week.

- Share one honest insight with someone you trust — let connection be part of your healing.
- If you feel overwhelmed, start small. Just trace the Choices and Triggers. Even that opens clarity.

Remember:
- This isn't a test. It's a conversation — with the part of you that's been trying to speak for a long time.
- Sometimes clarity begins when you stop trying to fix the symptom — and start tracing its roots.

Pause and reflect

Take a moment. Breathe deeply. And let these questions meet you honestly — not with pressure, but with presence.
This is not about fixing.
It's about facing the patterns that have quietly shaped your wellbeing.

1 – When you look at the patterns in your symptoms, what connections do you notice?
Are they tied to certain times, people, responsibilities, or roles you perform?

2 – Which habits or people consistently leave your body tense or drained?
Be specific. Patterns live in repetition. Clarity begins when you name what repeats.

3 – How does your body react when you override its signals?
Do you become anxious, numb, irritable, exhausted? How long does it take to recover?

4 – How would your life change if you respected your body as valid data – not noise, not weakness, but truth?
What decisions might shift? What boundaries might appear?

5 – What is one pattern you're ready to start acknowledging?
Not to change it yet – just to see it clearly, without excuse.

Write freely. Let what's true rise.
This reflection isn't about doing more. It's about seeing deeper.
Because once you connect the dots, you can't unsee them. And from that place, real choice begins.

CONTEXT Map worksheet

You'll find the CONTEXT Map worksheet in the OsteoLife LUCKY Toolkit at the back of this book. Use it to trace the invisible threads between your symptoms and your daily life.
Map what's been automatic.
Track what's been overwhelming.
Name what your body has been trying to reveal.

It's not about perfection – it's about pattern recognition. The more you practise, the clearer the story becomes.
Because, your body doesn't forget what your mind dismisses.
The CONTEXT Map helps you remember.

Chapter 4 tool recap

- **CONTEXT Map** – Use it weekly to trace patterns between your symptoms and your lived experience.
- **Weekly check-in practice** – Take 10 minutes to connect the dots between what you do and what you feel.
- **Reflection question:** What patterns in my environment or routines shape how my body feels?

Use these tools not to diagnose, but to understand.

Because clarity isn't found in control – it's found in connection.

Invitation

If connecting the dots feels like opening a door you've kept shut, take it one step at a time. You don't have to untangle everything today. You only need to begin.

Awareness doesn't demand perfection – it asks for presence.

It's not about overhauling your life overnight. It's about noticing the quiet thread that runs through your choices, your symptoms, and your story.

When you start to see your patterns, you start to reclaim your power. Because what you can see, you can shift.

In the next chapter, we'll explore how to meet these insights with compassion, and how to build rituals of kindness that anchor you when things feel overwhelming.

We'll look at how to create support – not just strategies – for the version of you that's learning to come home to your body.

You've listened. You've understood. And you've connected.

Now, it's time to offer care.

Let's begin.

CHAPTER 5

Kindness

> *Create rituals to be kind to your body and respect your limits*

These rituals are acts of kindness to your body and yourself, creating space to heal and grow

What does it mean to practise kindness?

You've learnt to listen – to hear the signals your body has been sending.
You've learnt to understand – to interpret the patterns beneath the pain.
You've learnt to connect – to see how every ache, every symptom, every tight breath fits into a larger truth.
Now comes the most misunderstood, most often skipped, and yet most essential layer: kindness.

This step isn't soft. It's not indulgent. It's not about bubble baths or taking a break from 'being hard on yourself'.

Kindness is the skill that turns insight into transformation.

It's the daily decision to treat your body, not as something to overcome, but as something to honour.

Because here's what no one teaches you:

- Awareness without reinforcement fades.
- Understanding without care creates guilt.
- Connection without compassion becomes pressure.

Kindness is the glue.

It's what allows change to stick – not just for a few days, but for the long haul.

It means meeting yourself with respect, especially:
- on the days when your habits fall apart
- in the moments when shame creeps in
- when you feel like you're not enough, or doing enough.

Your body has worked tirelessly to protect you. To keep going. To adapt. Even when ignored. Even when overridden. Even when silenced.

Kindness is how you say: 'I see you now. I hear you. I'm here to stay.'
Your body is not a burden to manage. It is your most loyal ally. It is the reason you're still here.

Let's start treating it like that.

Not once in a while. But every day – especially on the days you forget how far you've come. Because this isn't about being 'nice', it's about being true and showing up for yourself – not only when you've earned it, but simply because **you're worth it.**

Why does kindness matter?

Kindness matters because most people don't struggle to begin. They struggle to continue.
They set intentions with fire. Then life intervenes – with fatigue, with failure, and with fear.
And when things slip, their instinct isn't support.
It's shame.
Punishment.
Abandonment.

Kindness is what interrupts that spiral.
It gives you something to return to when your plan unravels, when discipline disappears, or when perfection is no longer an option.

Without kindness, you treat your body like a project.
With it, you treat your body like a relationship.

And relationships are sustained by how we respond. Not in moments of triumph, but in moments of tenderness.

Because transformation isn't forged in force. It's sustained by the way you speak to yourself when everything feels hard.

This is why kindness matters: it's not a reward for getting it right – it's the reason you keep going when it all goes wrong.

When does kindness matter most?

Kindness matters most in the moments you were taught to abandon yourself.

When you fall behind, lose momentum, or your best intentions dissolve into old habits. Especially when the voice in your head says: 'You don't deserve it.'

That's the moment kindness becomes essential – not earned, but necessary.

Not when you're thriving. Not when everything feels aligned. But when you're tired, reactive, or disconnected. When you do the thing you said you'd stop doing. When your body whispers 'I'm not okay', and your instinct is to push through anyway.

Kindness isn't what comes after success. It's what makes success sustainable.

It's the part that says that you don't have to be perfect to be worthy of care.

You don't have to get it right to begin again. Because lasting change never starts with pressure.

It begins when you learn how to stay – especially when things fall apart.

Where does kindness live?

Kindness doesn't wait for the perfect moment, but lives in the unnoticed ones.

It lives in the breath you take before answering the email that drains you, in the stretch you allow yourself between back-to-back meetings, in the choice to eat slowly instead of rushing through lunch at your desk, and in the moment you catch yourself saying, 'You're behind again,' and instead whisper, 'You're doing your best.'

You don't need to overhaul your life.
You need to stop abandoning yourself in the name of performance.
Kindness isn't the grand gesture. It's the micro-rescue.

It lives in the small, consistent places where you choose to respond rather than retreat. To soothe rather than scold. To come home to yourself rather than power through.

This is how change becomes sustainable.
Not through pressure. But through presence.

How do you start?

You don't start kindness with willpower.

You start with what's real – the energy you have, the resistance you feel, the life you're actually living. This is where the **STAY Map**™ comes in.

It is not another rigid plan. Not another system to fail. But a repeatable ritual that anchors you when everything else feels uncertain.

Because life will get messy. Your schedule will break. Your energy will dip. And the habits that will survive those moments are the ones built on respect, not rigidity.

The STAY Map helps you create habits that hold, even on your hardest day. You don't need more discipline. You need a way to stay with yourself.

My experience

For me, kindness didn't begin as a concept. It began as survival. I didn't even realise I was practising it.

When I moved from France to Australia, the transition was more than just a change of address – it was a full-body upheaval. It was a new culture, a new environment, and new responsibilities. My nervous system felt like it was constantly bracing.

Back in France, my menstrual cycle was uneventful. No pain or noticeable mood shifts. But after the move, that changed. Each month I felt waves of irritability and emotional overwhelm I'd never known before.

My period became a storm – not just physically, but mentally. I didn't know what was happening. I just knew I needed relief.

So I did something that made no sense on paper – but that felt intuitively right.

I started swimming in the ocean. All year round.

At first it was just a way to breathe. A moment away from the noise, the pressure, the constant 'holding it all together'.

But something shifted.

My body began to respond – not with resistance, but with release. My premenstrual symptoms eased, and my stress dropped. Even during university exams, a time that would normally trigger anxiety, I felt… steady, calm, present.

My body wasn't fighting me anymore. And it clicked.

This ritual of cold water, movement, and stillness – was **kindness in action**.

It didn't look like a spa day.

And it didn't come with a label.

It came from **listening to what my body needed**… and choosing to respond.

That's when I realised that you might already be practising kindness – you just haven't named it yet.

If something in your life is easing your symptoms… if your anxiety quiets, your pain lessens, your sleep deepens…

That's your body saying: 'Thank you.'

Kindness isn't always dramatic. Sometimes it looks like cold water, bare skin, and breath. Sometimes it's the one thing that makes everything else more bearable.

And that's how you know it's working.

The STAY Map

Use this as a simple guide to create sustainable rituals that support your wellbeing:

S – Start stupidly small	What tiny step can you take – even on your hardest day?
T – Tie it to something you already do	What existing habit can you link this new ritual to?
A – Allow for imperfection	How will you show kindness when you forget or resist?
Y – Yes, celebrate small wins	What moments of presence and effort can you notice and appreciate?

Apply this to building one new ritual – and you'll begin to stay consistent through compassion, not pressure.

Let's dive deeper.

S – Start stupidly small

Start so small it feels almost laughable. So small you can do it even on your hardest, most chaotic day.
One breath before your emails. One sentence in your journal. One moment of stillness between tasks.
Small is sustainable. Small is how you stay.

T – Tie it to something you already do

Your life is already full, so don't add more – anchor it.
Link the ritual to something you already do every day: brushing your teeth, boiling the kettle, or starting your car.
It doesn't have to be new. It just needs to be yours.

A – Allow for imperfection

You will forget. You will resist. And you will miss days.
That's not failure. That's life.
Kindness means planning for the mess, not punishing yourself when it comes.
Progress isn't measured in perfect streaks – it's in how gently you return.

Y – Yes, celebrate small wins

Don't celebrate with fanfare – but with presence.
You noticed. You paused. You showed up.
That matters.
Celebrating the effort, not the outcome, rewires your brain and body for trust.
It's how consistency becomes a reflex, not a demand.

Why this matters

These steps are deceptively simple, but don't confuse simplicity with weakness.
It's easier to chase perfect plans than to meet yourself with compassion.
It's easier to control than to care.
But only one of those creates rituals that last.

Kindness isn't soft – it's a strategy.
And this is how you make it real.

Real stories – kindness in action

In this chapter, we share real stories that illuminate the gentle power of kindness in healing and transformation. Witness how small, deliberate acts and mindful attention can rebuild trust – both with ourselves and others.

These stories are concise yet deeply relatable, reminding us that kindness is not grand gestures alone but often the quiet, consistent moments that open the way to presence and connection. They show how tiny, compassionate steps can guide us from control and precision towards heartfelt presence, creating space for growth and self-acceptance.

From precision to presence

Elise, 47, was a sharp, driven entrepreneur running a high-performing business while managing a busy family life. From the outside she exuded control. Internally, she was unravelling.

'I do everything right,' she said, shoulders tight, voice flat. 'But it still doesn't feel like enough.'

Her body was pleading for attention. She had:
- chronic bloating
- fatigue masked by caffeine
- emotional volatility she couldn't explain.

Like most high-performers, her first instinct was to double down. To fix it and do more. To be better. But her system was already maxed out.

When we introduced the STAY Map, she dismissed it. 'Small steps won't fix this,' she said.

But we began anyway, with one simple act: to eat one meal a day with no distractions.

Not perfectly, just consistently.
She resisted. Then she softened.
And slowly, the signals started making sense.
She saw the link between her flared symptoms and toxic client interactions.
She realised her 'healthy meals' were eaten tense, standing, between tasks.
She saw how her body never had a chance to rest – even while she ate.

So we made space for care:
- She moved her desk to a quieter spot.
- She scheduled 15-minute breath breaks between calls.
- She started eating lunch screen-free, with presence.

Her digestion improved and her mood evened out. But more than anything – **she stopped believing she had to earn rest by being perfect.**

What changed for Elise?

- She chose presence over pressure.
- She swapped performance for permission.
- She honoured her limits instead of resenting them.

Lessons learnt

- Kindness creates consistency.
- Small wins are scalable.
- You can't resent your body into resilience.

How is Elise now?

Elise has shifted from pushing harder to leading with presence and permission. By adopting simple, consistent practices like mindful, screen-free meals and scheduled breath breaks, she reduced internal tension and improved her physical symptoms.

Instead of resisting her limits, she learned to honour them, creating space for care that stabilised her energy and emotional balance. This aligned leadership – choosing kindness and small wins over relentless performance – helped her rebuild sustainable resilience without burning out.

Relearning trust through tiny steps

Mia, 45, had built her identity in the pressure cooker of high-end kitchens. She had Michelin stars, award-winning menus, and a reputation built on excellence.

Perfection wasn't optional – it was the culture. And her body was collapsing under it.

She had chronic pain, sleepless nights, and panic attacks that gripped her at 3am.

'I've tried everything,' she said in our first session. 'Acupuncture, supplements, and therapy. But nothing sticks. It's like I can't hold on to change.'

She didn't believe small steps could do anything.

So we started with one that seemed almost ridiculous: one minute of breathing before checking her phone in the morning.

'That's it?' she asked, unimpressed.

'Yes,' I said. 'That's it.'

She rolled her eyes – but she did it. And slowly, it shifted everything.

That minute became a pause she could count on.

Her jaw softened, and her breath deepened. She stopped launching into the day like a battle. She added a single stretch after each shift. Then a pause before walking into the kitchen. Then a quiet check-in: 'What do I need right now?'

It was nothing dramatic; nothing Instagram-worthy.
But it was real, consistent, and kind.
And her body noticed.
Her pain quieted. Her sleep returned. Her panic lost its grip.
Not because she forced herself to be better – **but because she finally allowed herself to be human.**

What changed for Mia?

- She stopped viewing rest as weakness.
- She let care – not control – guide her rituals.
- She built a system that matched her energy, not her ego.

Lessons learnt

- Self-respect makes healing sustainable.
- Gentleness is a form of wisdom.
- Safety begins in how you treat yourself.

How is Mia now?

Mia has shifted from relentless perfectionism towards a sustainable, gentle rhythm of self-care. By committing to small, consistent pauses – starting with just one minute of intentional breathing each morning – she retrained her body and mind to respond with less pain, better sleep, and reduced panic.

Her healing isn't about force or quick fixes but about building a kind, realistic relationship with herself that honours her human limits rather than her ego's demands.

Try this today – the STAY reset

Sustainable change doesn't begin with intensity – it begins with consistency. And consistency is built on rituals you can actually return to, even on your worst day. Use the STAY Map to build one tiny ritual of care.

S – Start stupidly small

Start so small it feels almost silly.
Take one deep breath before replying to a message. Write one sentence in your journal. Put one hand on your heart before sleep.
Start where resistance can't argue.

T – Tie it to a routine

Anchor your ritual to something you already do. While brushing your teeth, boiling the jug, or locking your car.
This creates frictionless repetition.

A – Allow imperfection

You will miss a day. That's not failure – it's feedback.
The ritual isn't there to test your discipline. It's there to help you *return*.
Return with grace. Return with self-respect.

Y – Yes, celebrate

Celebrate the doing – not the scale of the result.
Acknowledge the effort: 'I showed up.'
Because your brain needs to feel it matters – so it repeats it again tomorrow.

Optional practice

- Write your ritual on a sticky note and place it where you'll see it.
- Set a gentle reminder – your phone, a Post-it note, or your planner.
- At the end of the week, pause and ask: 'What shifted when I treated myself with consistent care?'

This isn't about building a perfect routine. It's about building a *relationship* – with yourself.

And every time you show up, even for one breath, you're telling your body: 'You matter to me.'

Pause and reflect

Before you move forward, take a moment to be still.

These questions aren't to check your performance. They're for honesty. For clarity. For you.

- **What's one tiny act of care you could begin today?**
  Not the most impressive – just the most doable.

- **Where do you notice yourself holding back, even when you want to fully show up?**
  In your tone, your body, or the way you schedule time for yourself?

- **What emotion surfaces when you allow imperfection?**
  Is it a relief? Shame? Resistance? Name it – so it doesn't own you.

- **What would your routines look like if they were designed for support, not control?**
  Would they soften your day – or structure your worth?

- **How would it feel to let kindness lead?**
  Not just when things go well – but especially when they don't.

This is the moment to pause – not to judge, but to observe.
Because awareness is the doorway.
Kindness is the key.

STAY Map worksheet

Refer to the OsteoLife LUCKY Toolkit at the back of this book for the STAY Map worksheet and habit builder.

Use it to:
- design rituals that meet your real life – not your ideal one
- track the habits that hold you, especially on hard days
- build momentum rooted in self-respect, not self-judgement.

Consistency doesn't come from pressure. It comes from structure that's kind enough to stay.

Chapter 5 tool recap

- **STAY Map** – Build micro-rituals that hold, even when life doesn't
- **Weekly ritual builder** – Design habits rooted in care, not control
- **Reflection question:** What's one supportive practice I can keep – even when everything else changes?

Kindness isn't what you add when things are calm.
It's what you return to when everything else falls away.

Invitation

Kindness is not a backup plan. It's the architecture of staying.
It's the voice that whispers, 'You're still worthy', even when your plans fall apart.

It's how your body learns to trust you again.
Not because you never fall, but because you always return.

If listening helped you notice, understanding helped you name, connecting helped you see the patterns, and kindness helped you stay, now comes the step that turns awareness into embodiment: action.
Not the frantic kind. Not the performative kind.
But aligned action – rooted in what you now know to be true.

Because once you've heard your body, understood its signals, and built rituals of support, you're ready to move – not from urgency, but from grounded intention.

In the next chapter, you'll learn how to act –
With clarity.
With power.
With alignment.

This is where momentum begins.

Next, we complete the journey with Y: You take action.

CHAPTER 6

You take action

Your journey from awareness to taking action

You've listened. You've understood. You've connected. And you've built rituals that meet you where you are – not where you 'should' be. And slowly, your body has begun to trust you again.

But insight, no matter how profound, is only the beginning.

Real change lives in what happens next.

This is the chapter most people avoid – not because they don't want change, but because they fear they won't get it right.

But this isn't about getting it right. It's about showing up, again and again, with respect.

Because the truth is: you can't think your way into transformation.

You have to act your way into alignment.

The smallest step taken with self-respect will always move you further than the grandest plan fuelled by self-judgement.

This chapter is not about perfection. It's about devotion. To your needs. To your boundaries. To the truth your body keeps trying to tell you.

And when you take action from that place – not to fix yourself, but to honour yourself – everything begins to shift

What does it mean to take action with respect?

Action rooted in respect is quiet, steady, and deeply personal.
It doesn't shout. It doesn't rush.
It listens – then responds with care.

Taking action with respect means you stop treating your body like a problem to be solved, and start treating it like a voice to be honoured.

It's not about overhauling your life overnight. It's about one choice, one shift, one boundary that says: 'I hear you. And I'm willing to change because you matter.'

This isn't a reaction – it's a response.
Not from fear. Not from guilt. But from grounded clarity.
It's the moment you realise that ignoring your needs is no longer an option.
Because every time you act from respect, you build trust.
And trust is what creates the safety needed for true change to last.

Why does taking action matter?

Awareness without action becomes a weight.
You can notice and understand all the signs your body gives you. But if you don't take action, you just stay stuck – knowing a lot but not making any changes.

That's when the ache gets louder. Not just the ache in your body, but the ache of self-betrayal.

You know the cycle. You see the pattern. And still, you override it.

It's not only the feelings you notice in your body that wear you out, but also the quiet space afterwards when you don't understand what they mean.

Respectful action is how you close that gap. It's how you turn knowing into becoming. It's how you rebuild the bridge between intention and integrity.

Because the longer you wait to act, the more you teach your body it can't count on you. But every small step – done with respect, not urgency – says: I'm listening. I'm here. I won't abandon you this time.

That's what makes this moment matter.

It's not about doing everything.
It's about doing one thing – and letting that be enough to start

Where does action happen?

Action doesn't just happen in your mind. Or in the journal where you had the breakthrough. Or in the therapy room or the yoga mat.

Action lives in the places where your life unfolds – messy, real, and unfiltered.

It lives in:
- the words you say – and the ones you finally stop saying
- the boundaries you hold – and the unspoken tensions you no longer accept
- the habits you build – not for productivity, but for peace
- the spaces you choose to enter – and the ones you decide to leave.

Action is not a performance.

It's a translation of what you now *know* into what you now *do*. It's the moment you put down your phone instead of numbing out. The moment you say 'no' without explanation. The moment you leave the conversation, the job, the room – because your body said *enough*.

This is where the inner work becomes visible. Where clarity stops being potential and becomes momentum.

Because if it doesn't actually happen in your life, it's not transformation. It's a theory.

When should you act?

Act when your body whispers something it's already said a hundred times.
When the symptom is no longer surprising – but persistent.
When the pattern is clear – but you keep tolerating it anyway.
When the voice in your head says, 'I know this isn't good for me', and the next moment you ignore it again.

These are not signs of failure. They are thresholds, invitations, turning points.
They are the moments when silence starts to cost too much.

Action doesn't wait for the perfect time. It waits for your *honesty*. The moment you admit what's no longer working – not with shame, but with courage.

That's when something shifts.
Not because you fix it all at once, but because you decide: 'This time, I'll do something different.'
Even if it's small. Even if it's just one boundary.
One breath. One 'No'. One truth finally named.
That's when action begins – not when you feel ready, but when you finally choose to respect what you already know.

How do you start?

You start with the smallest step your nervous system can trust.
Not the one that looks impressive. Or the one that proves your worth.
But the one that says, 'I'm listening' – and 'I'm ready'.

Change doesn't begin with pressure. It begins with presence.
The **ACTION Map**™ gives structure to the swirl of insight you've gathered.
It turns awareness into movement – one respectful choice at a time.

Action doesn't require you to have it all figured out. It only asks you to begin.
You don't need a five-year plan. You don't need a 30-day challenge.
You need one act of alignment. Today.
Not from urgency. But from truth. From care. From the quiet decision that your healing deserves follow-through.
That's how you start.

My experience

For a long time I believed taking action meant getting everything perfect. Maybe it's the Virgo in me – perfectionism was practically my second language.

If I could just crack the code – perfect routines, perfect sleep schedule, perfect boundaries – I thought I would finally feel calm in my body.

So I did what high-achievers do. I made plans. I built routines. I colour-coded every area of my life. I set rigid goals and told myself, 'This time I'll never fall behind.'

And for a few days, I felt the high of progress. Until life happened.

I would have a client crisis, a sleepless night, or a family emergency.

And just like that, it all fell apart.

Then came the shame. 'You see? You never stick to anything.'

At the time I thought my issue was discipline. But what I eventually realised was that my issue was *scale*.

I was trying to overhaul everything at once… from fear. Fear that if I didn't do it all, I'd never feel better. Fear that if I let go of control, everything would fall apart.

One night, after yet another failed attempt to 'fix my life', I sat at my kitchen table – surrounded by lists, highlighters, and guilt – and felt the weight of emptiness.

That's when a quieter question surfaced: What is the smallest action I could take that would feel like respect – and maybe even love?

The answer was not dramatic. It wasn't a program, a challenge, or a reinvention.

It was simple: shut my laptop by 8pm every night – for one week.

At first, it felt too small to matter. But I did it.

The first night, I was twitchy. My brain kept whispering, 'Check your emails.'

But by night three, something shifted. My breath slowed. My body softened. My sleep deepened.

And most of all – I felt relief.

I had finally chosen an action that was built for *me*, not for the version of me I thought I 'should' be.

That one act of love made the next one easier. Not because I was suddenly more disciplined. But because I finally understood: action doesn't have to be big to be life-changing.

It has to be honest. It has to be consistent. And it has to come from care – not control.

That's why I created the **ACTION Map** to remind myself (and now you) that real change isn't forced.

It's chosen.

One small, respectful step at a time.

The ACTION Map

Use this as a simple guide to respectful, sustainable change — one small step at a time:

A – Address one thing at a time	What is the loudest need demanding your attention right now?
C – Choose the smallest effective change	What tiny shift feels doable and respectful, not pressured?
T – Test, don't commit	What if you tried this just as an experiment for one week?
I – Iterate based on results	What worked? What didn't? How can you adjust kindly?
O – Optimise what works	What nourishes you and deserves more time and energy?
N – Never stop experimenting	What new step are you curious to try next?

Apply this to one change at a time — and you'll move forward with clarity, compassion, and consistency.

Let's dive deeper.

A – Address one thing at a time

Start where the pain is loudest or the need is clearest.

Choose one area – not ten. Your nervous system can only process so much at once.
Ask yourself: What's one part of my life that's asking for attention right now?

C – Choose the smallest effective change

Pick something so doable that it almost feels too small.
One pause. One breath. One 'No'.
Because the goal is not size – it's sustainability.
Ask yourself: What shift would feel like respect, not pressure?

T – Test, don't commit

Don't make lifelong promises or rigid plans.
Try it for one week. That's it.
Curiosity is more powerful than control.
Ask yourself: What happens if I try this for seven days – just as an experiment?

I – Iterate based on results

Reflect. Observe. And adjust.
If it works, keep going. If it doesn't, you haven't failed – you've learnt.
Ask yourself: What helped me feel more supported? What didn't?

O – Optimise what works

Double down on what feels nourishing. Let go of what doesn't.
Build momentum from what's already working.
Ask yourself: What felt easier than expected? Can I do more of that?

N – Never stop experimenting

This isn't a finish line. It's a relationship – with your body, with your needs, and with your truth.
Stay open. Keep evolving.
Ask yourself: What's one new thing I'm curious to try next?

Even the smallest action, done with respect, becomes a practice of self-trust.
You don't need to force transformation.
You just need to start where you are – and stay honest about what's true.

Real stories – you in action

In this chapter, the real stories bring to life the transformative power of taking intentional action – shifting from silence to self-respect and reclaiming calm in just one minute. These stories are designed to be clear, concise, and impactful, much like a compelling life story told in under a minute.

You will see how deliberate, focused attention in critical moments creates breakthrough shifts. These moments remind us that action, when guided by presence and clarity, can spark profound inner change and restore balance even in the busiest or most challenging times.

From silence to self-respect

Sophie, 49, was a client I'd worked with for years. She was the kind of woman others described as grounded – steady, thoughtful, and deeply attuned.

But the day she first walked in, her shoulders were locked and her jaw clenched so tight it hurt to speak. Something was different. She didn't need to say it, her body already had.

In fragments, her story came out.

She'd seen an old friend the night before – someone she'd known for decades. A friend who always left her doubting herself.

'I feel like it's my fault,' she whispered, tears brimming. 'Like I'm too sensitive. Like I should just let it go.'

We didn't start with fixing the friendship. We started with her body.

We used the **ACTION Map** to decode the tension in her chest.

She traced it back – not just to the conversation, but to years of shrinking herself to keep the peace. The ache wasn't just about that one friend. It was about a lifetime of overriding her own discomfort.

Her first action wasn't confrontation. It was a presence.

For two weeks she practised this one question before reacting: 'What do I need right now?'

The answer was simple: to be heard and respected.

When she finally spoke with her friend – not from rage, but from clarity – something unexpected happened. Her friend didn't argue. She listened.

The change wasn't in the friend.

It was in Sophie.

What changed for Sophie?

- She stopped outsourcing her worth to others' approval.
- She honoured her discomfort as valid communication.
- She chose calm, clear action over self-silencing.

Lessons learnt

- Respectful action begins with honest awareness.
- You don't need permission to honour your truth.
- Boundaries often begin in the body.

How is Sophie now?

Sophie is in a stronger, more grounded place than before. By tuning in to her body's signals and asking, 'What do I need right now?' she shifted from self-silencing to owning her worth without needing others' approval.

This daily practice of presence helped her approach difficult conversations with calm clarity instead of reactive frustration. Her boundaries are now embodied and clear – rooted in self-respect rather than external validation. Sophie no longer waits for crises or anger to take action; she trusts her discomfort as meaningful guidance and feels aligned with her own truth.

Reclaiming calm in one minute

Daniel, 35, was a gifted graphic designer with a sharp eye for detail but a quiet storm of anxiety beneath the surface.

He spoke with precision, but his body told a different story. He had a tight chest, clenched jaw, and shallow breath.

'It's like I'm always bracing,' he said. 'Waiting for something to go wrong.'

He was in a cycle of quiet survival. He was tense before emails, and wired before deadlines. He was exhausted, but still pushing.

He didn't need more insight – he needed a shift.

We started with something he almost dismissed entirely: one minute.

Just one breath before opening his laptop each morning. 'It doesn't feel like enough,' he said. But he did it anyway.

And something started to shift. The pause gave him space.

He used it before checking emails, before starting projects, and before replying in frustration.

One minute became a pattern of presence. Not dramatic, but real.

His breath deepened, his jaw softened, and his reactivity eased. For the first time in years he wasn't just managing stress – he was relating to himself differently.

He stopped seeing his body as the battleground. He began to see it as his barometer. His guide.

What changed for Daniel?

- He stopped waiting for the perfect moment to act.
- He embraced consistency over intensity.
- He reclaimed his body as an ally – not an obstacle.

Lessons learnt

- Gentle actions create lasting change.
- Self-respect builds through daily choices.
- Even one breath can shift your direction.

How is Daniel now?

Daniel is doing significantly better. By committing to the simple practice of one mindful breath each morning and before stressful moments, he shifted from constant bracing to a state of presence. His physical tension has eased – his breath deepens naturally, his jaw relaxes, and his overall reactivity has diminished.

Instead of surviving anxious cycles, he now relates to his body as a trusted guide and ally. This new rhythm has fostered self-respect built through daily, gentle choices rather than waiting for dramatic change.

If you're waiting for the big shift, pause.
Your body doesn't need perfection – it needs presence.
Start where you are. Choose one breath. One act. One return.
That's how momentum begins.

Try this today – daily ACTION check (experiment)

Choose one area where you feel stuck – physically, emotionally, or mentally. Then walk it through the **ACTION Map**.

A – Address one thing at a time

What's the single issue or pattern that feels most present right now? Start there.

C – Choose the smallest effective change

Ask yourself: What's one shift I could make that feels doable, and not overwhelming?

T – Test, don't commit

Try it for one week – not forever. Just enough to notice what happens.

I – Iterate based on results

At the end of the week, reflect. What helped? What got in the way? Adjust.

O – Optimise what works

If something supports you – amplify it. Let it become part of your rhythm.

N – Never stop experimenting

There is no final version of healing. Keep evolving with curiosity.

Optional practice

- At the end of the day, jot down one action you took and how it felt in your body.
- Choose one way to celebrate – no matter how small. Acknowledgement is momentum.

Remember:
- You don't need the perfect plan.
- You just need one step that feels like self-respect.

Pause and reflect

Take a moment. Breathe. Be honest.

- What emotion rises when you think about taking action – not out of pressure, but out of care?
- What's one small change your body is quietly asking for right now?
- How do you usually respond when you slip or break a habit? With shame… or with grace?
- What would it look like to act – not to fix yourself – but to *honour* yourself?
- What's one way you can celebrate consistency, not just outcomes?

This is where change begins.
Not in the plan. But in the pause.

ACTION Map worksheet

Refer to the OsteoLife LUCKY Toolkit at the back of this book for the ACTION Map worksheet.

Use it to track your experiments, reflect on what shifted, and refine your next step – not from pressure, but from partnership.

One small, respectful action at a time.

Chapter 6 tool recap

- **ACTION Map** – Start with one focus.
- **Weekly action review** – Build momentum through reflection.
- **Reflection question:** What small, respectful action is my body asking you to take today?

Invitation

If taking action feels vulnerable, know this: every small step is a declaration that you are worth caring for.

It's not about proving anything. It's about choosing to meet yourself – not with pressure, but with presence. Because your body doesn't need perfection. It needs partnership.

In the next chapter, we'll explore what this journey looks like for women in leadership – where your body carries not just your story, but the weight of every expectation you've ever been asked to meet.

Let's name it.

Let's honour it.

Let's lead differently – starting with the body.

This is where embodiment becomes real. Now, we apply it – especially in leadership.

CHAPTER 7

Leading from Alignment

For Women who put everyone first, now it's time to breathe

For women who lead others, alignment begins with leading yourself. This is your invitation to lead from within.

This chapter isn't about tips to 'balance it all.'
It's a reclamation. Of your presence. Of your voice. Of your body as a compass – not an obstacle – in how you lead.

Because leadership rooted in self-abandonment isn't sustainable.
And power built on burnout isn't power – it's survival.

This is your invitation to lead from a place that's honest.
To align with what strengthens you – not drains you.

To remember: your capacity to lead others is directly connected to your capacity to stay connected to yourself.

What does it mean to lead from alignment?

To lead from alignment means staying rooted in yourself – even when the world asks you to disconnect. It means treating your inner signals as data, not distractions. It means trusting that your body is not a liability to manage – but a compass to lead with.

When you lead from alignment, you:
- show up with presence, not performance
- respond with clarity, not compliance
- move with courage, not depletion.

It's not about leading perfectly.
It's about leading truthfully – from a place that sustains you, not silences you.

Why does leading from alignment matter?

This matters because abandoning yourself to meet expectations comes at a double cost.

First, your body absorbs it – through tension, headaches, and sleepless nights. Then, your leadership reflects it – through reactivity, resentment, and burnout.

Leadership without alignment is just performance. It might appear strong – but it fractures you over time.

You can't lead others with clarity if you're disconnected from yourself.

Your greatest influence doesn't come from how much you carry. It comes from how deeply you're grounded.

And that begins with leading yourself – first, fully, and consistently.

When should you reconnect?

Reconnect the moment leadership starts weighing you down from the inside out.

When your shoulders stay tense long after the meeting ends. When you're absorbing everyone else's stress – but ignoring your own. When you're performing with calmness on the outside, while quietly unravelling within.

These moments aren't failures. They're signals.

They are not a call to push harder – but an invitation to return to yourself.

Reconnection isn't a luxury. It's the reset that makes your next step sustainable.

Where does this happen?

Alignment lives in the micro-moments no one applauds: the inhale before walking into a boardroom where you'll be challenged, the exhale after holding space for everyone but yourself, and the pause when your name is called and you must choose between presence or performance.

It happens in hallways. In your car. At your desk.

Not in grand gestures – but in quiet choices that bring you back to yourself.

You don't need more time. You need more truth. You need permission to feel – before you lead.

That's where real alignment begins.

How do you start?

Use the **ALIGN Map**™ for a grounded daily practice to reconnect – before the demands, the meetings, the noise.

It's not another item on your list. It's a moment of return. A recalibration that anchors you in your body – before the world asks for more of you. The ALIGN Map helps you pause with intention, lead with clarity, and act without abandoning yourself.

My experience

For years, I believed I was immune to burnout. I loved my work, I was purpose-driven, and I had built something that mattered.

But meaning doesn't cancel out exhaustion. And passion doesn't protect you if you never pause to reconnect.

As a woman leading my own clinic, I carried an invisible weight: to be the anchor, to perform steadiness, and to absorb pressure without breaking stride.

I had internalised the myths handed to so many high-capacity women that strength means silence, that capability means invincibility and that if people rely on you, rest is no longer an option.

I pushed through weeks of hormonal headaches and bone-deep fatigue. I smiled through brain fog. I held space for others while quietly slipping out of relationship with myself.

Until one Friday evening, after back-to-back clients and another demanding cycle, I sat alone in my kitchen, holding a cold mug of tea.

And I heard it clearly: **'I'm tired of pretending I'm fine.'**

That moment didn't change everything. But it changed me. Because I finally told the truth – not out loud, but inwardly.

If I kept pushing like this I would lose the very capacity that made me effective. And I remembered the line we all nod to during flight safety briefings: **put your own mask on first.** Except, women forget that in leadership and life, the mask exists too.

That insight became the seed of the ALIGN Map: a structured way to check in – especially when I didn't have time to fix everything. It is a moment to reset – even when life didn't pause for me. A way to lead from wholeness – not just habit.

I still face hard weeks. But I no longer see them as problems to fix.

I see them as feedback. As invitations to return.

Because leadership from alignment doesn't require perfection.

It requires presence.

And the willingness to stop abandoning yourself in the name of being *strong*.

The ALIGN Map

Use this as a simple daily reset for whole-body leadership:

A – Acknowledge	What is your body communicating right now?
L – Locate	Where do you feel it – jaw, chest, gut, shoulders?
I – Inquire	What is this sensation trying to tell you? What need or boundary?
G – Ground	How can you reset with intention – breath, stretch, stillness?
N – Navigate	What is one aligned action that honours your body and values?

Apply this each day – and you'll recalibrate your presence, leading yourself with clarity in every moment.

Let's dive deeper.

A – Acknowledge

Notice what your body is communicating – for example, tension, fatigue, or restlessness.
Don't rush to fix it – just name it. Naming is the first act of leadership.

L – Locate

Where does the sensation live in your body?

Jaw? Chest? Gut? Shoulders?

Anchor your awareness there. That's where your truth is surfacing.

I – Inquire

What is this feeling trying to reveal?
Is there a boundary being crossed? A need unmet?
Curiosity is how you translate sensation into insight.

G – Ground

Reset with intention.
Take a breath. Stretch. Be still.
Let your body know it's safe to recalibrate.

N – Navigate

Move forward from alignment, not reaction.
What's one action that honours both your body and your leadership values?

Even though these steps take less than a minute, they recalibrate your presence.
Because, how you lead yourself in the micro-moments determines how you lead everything else.

Real stories – alignment in action

This chapter shares real stories that showcase the evolution of leadership through self-awareness and aligned action. These narratives reveal how effective leaders move beyond reactive control towards grounded presence and clear priorities.

The stories demonstrate that authentic leadership requires setting boundaries and making strategic commitments with conviction, not just pushing harder. They offer lessons on resilience, focus, and the power of saying no – crucial skills for leading with clarity and integrity in complex environments.

From bracing leadership to boundaries leadership

Laura, 55, was a finance executive overseeing nearly 100 people. On the outside she was composed, effective, and respected. But when she came to see me, she was silently running on empty.

Her boss – a brilliant yet relentlessly critical leader – left her bracing daily for disapproval. She couldn't sleep. Her jaw clenched so tightly each morning she struggled to eat.

I introduced her to the ALIGN Map. At first it felt too simple. But as she began pausing before meetings, noticing her breath, and anchoring into her own authority, something shifted.

She no longer mirrored her boss's urgency. She no longer shrank in anticipation of critique. She showed up grounded, and spoke with clarity.

And her boss – noticing the shift – responded with the one thing Laura had stopped expecting: respect.

Weeks later, she was promoted. Not because she became someone new – but because she finally backed herself.

'I didn't change how I work,' she said. 'I changed how I relate to myself.'

What changed for Laura?

- She stopped bracing against imagined criticism.
- She grounded herself before reacting.
- She reclaimed authority without sacrificing wellbeing.

Lessons learnt

- Your body always knows when you're betraying yourself for approval.
- Alignment isn't something you earn – it's something you practice.
- Respecting your limits is a form of leadership.

How is Laura now?

Laura is thriving in her leadership role with a renewed sense of authority grounded in self-alignment rather than reactive bracing. By practising presence through the ALIGN Map, she stopped shrinking from imagined criticism and instead showed up with calm clarity.

This shift not only improved her wellbeing but also transformed how others, including her boss, perceived and respected her. Her promotion came from this authentic confidence. She didn't change her work – she changed her relationship with herself.

This is how you lead without losing yourself.

Start where you are. One breath. One pause. One aligned choice at a time.

From overcommitment to embodied clarity

Helen, 43, was an HR consultant known for her calm, capable presence. But beneath the surface she was always bracing – anticipating everything that could go wrong. 'It's like my mind and body are in two different meetings,' she told me.

She lived in her head, solving problems, staying ahead, always saying yes.

When I introduced her to the ALIGN Map, she almost laughed. 'I don't have time to feel things,' she said.

But slowly, she started checking in. One breath before a meeting. One pause before replying. One question: Do I actually have the capacity for this?

She began to notice the reflex to overcommit. She noticed how often she said yes while her body said no.

Over time, she started choosing differently. Not because she became harder, but because she became clearer.

One day, a colleague said, 'You seem more grounded – like you actually trust yourself now.'

Helen didn't become less available. She became more aligned.

And in that shift, her leadership grew sharper – and more respected.

What changed for Helen?

- She stopped defaulting to overcommitment.
- She checked in before saying yes.
- She led with self-respect instead of self-sacrifice.

Lessons learnt

- Your worth is not measured by how much you can endure.
- Saying no is an act of leadership.
- When you pause to check in, you return to your own authority.

How is Helen now?

Helen has transformed her leadership by cultivating alignment with herself rather than pushing through overwhelm. Through small, consistent pauses and mindful capacity checks using the ALIGN Map, she shifted from automatic overcommitment to clear, respectful boundaries.

This new way of leading with self-respect – not sacrifice – has made her presence more grounded and sharpened her influence. Helen didn't gain a new external strategy; she rewired her internal relationship, embodying the leadership lesson that saying no and honouring limits is a powerful act.

This is what embodied leadership looks like.

Embodied leadership means first knowing and being with yourself – your feelings, strengths, and limits. This helps you speak honestly and connect with others' real fears and hopes, as we've seen. You don't have to be everywhere; focusing where you matter most avoids burnout and builds trust, a principle from general leadership advice.

Leadership is about understanding others' reasons ('why') and changing how you talk to fit their view. When you lead this way, from self-awareness and real connection, people listen and follow because it feels genuine and clear.

Try this today – the morning ALIGN

Before your day begins, take 60 seconds to lead from within.

A - Acknowledge what you feel.

Tension? Fatigue? Anticipation?

L - Locate where you feel it.

Jaw, chest, shoulders – notice where your body is speaking.

I - Inquire what it's telling you.

Is there a need you're ignoring? A boundary asking to be set?

G - Ground yourself with a breath, stretch, or pause.

Reset your nervous system before the day pulls you.

N - Navigate your next step.

What aligned action supports you right now?

Optional practice

Write one word on a sticky note that captures how you want to lead today – for example, clarity, steadiness, grace, or truth.

Let it guide you back to yourself when the day gets noisy.

Pause and reflect

Take a quiet moment to explore:

- What expectations have asked you to override your own needs?
- What signals does your body send when you're out of alignment?
- How might your leadership shift if you trusted your body's wisdom?
- What would become possible if you paused before responding?
- Where can you honour your limits – instead of pushing past them?

Let your answers guide you – not towards perfection, but towards presence.

Because leadership begins with listening to yourself first

ALIGN Map worksheet

Refer to the OsteoLife LUCKY Toolkit at the back of this book for your ALIGN Map worksheet.

Use it to reset, reflect, and lead from your centre – especially on the days that test you most.

Chapter 7 tool recap

- **ALIGN Map** – Daily reset for embodied leadership.

- **Morning ALIGN ritual** – Begin your day from clarity, not autopilot.

- **Reflection question:** What would change if I led from alignment – rather than expectation?

Invitation

If you've ever felt like your body was something to manage, hide, or apologise for – know this: you are not alone.

You were never the problem. Your body has always been your most honest ally.

Leading yourself with respect is not indulgent. It's intelligent. It's strategic. It's essential.

In the Conclusion, we'll bring everything together – so you can move forward with clarity, compassion, and grounded trust in yourself.

This isn't the end. It's the return – to your body, to your life, to your rhythm.

A real story from the OsteoLife LUCKY System in practice

You've seen how this journey begins. Now, here's how it continues – through those who've recently walked the LUCKY path.

Let this serve as both social proof and inspiration – real-time evidence that the system is active, relevant, and delivering results.

From burnout to boundaries

Louise, 49, was an executive manager navigating the pressures of a demanding leadership role, family responsibilities, and the constant pressure to 'keep it all together'. From the outside she looked like she was managing. But under the surface her body was sending warning signs – persistent pain in her ribs and shoulder, chronic stress, and the early signs of burnout.

She came into the OsteoLife LUCKY System thinking it might be just another stress-reduction method – some breathing, some mindfulness. What she found was far more confronting, and far more empowering.

'It pushed me to connect with my body,' she said, 'and to recognise that I'd been treating it like an enemy rather than a friend.'

That single shift – seeing her body as an ally, not a problem – changed everything.

Louise began to notice when stress showed up physically. Instead of overriding it, she paused, checked in, and responded differently.

'I'm more considered and less reactive,' she shared. 'I notice when people or situations trigger me. And I take care before I act.'

People around her noticed the shift too: 'You're calmer,' they said. 'Less reactive.'

What changed for Louise?

- She stopped placing herself last on the priority list.
- She shifted from self-criticism to self-awareness.
- She became more grounded, more present, and more in charge of her energy.

Lessons learnt

- Chronic stress isn't something to tolerate – it's something to translate.
- Burnout isn't just about doing too much – it's about disconnecting too often.
- True leadership starts with how you lead yourself.

How is Louise now?

Louise has made a powerful internal shift from battling her body to befriending it. Through the OsteoLife LUCKY System, she learned to translate chronic stress signals into actionable self-care, rather than pushing through pain and burnout.

This new relationship helps her lead with calm presence instead of pressure, checking in with her body's cues before reacting. While her responsibilities and pace remain demanding, her grounded presence and energy management have strengthened significantly, leading to greater resilience and sustainable leadership.

Final reflection

> *Coming home to your body*

You've done it.
You've returned. Back to the place you were never meant to leave: your body. Not by force. Not through pressure. But with presence.
By walking the path of the OsteoLife LUCKY System, you've done something radical: you've chosen partnership over punishment.

Here's what you've actually done:

You listened	to the whispers before they became screams
You understood	the messages beneath your symptoms
You connected	the dots between your habits, your environment, and your wellbeing
You chose kindness	by anchoring in sustainable rituals
You took action	from a place of self-respect and quiet strength
And for those who lead	you aligned your body with your mission

If there's one thing I want you to remember, it's this:

Your body is not a problem to solve.

It is your ally. Your home. Your most valuable asset.
It's not a machine to manage. Not a burden to override.
But the place you will live every moment of your life.

And I know…
That it's easy to forget. To believe productivity matters more than presence. That success requires self-sacrifice. That your worth must be proven by pushing through.
But you don't have to live like that anymore. You can choose a different way.

You can choose to meet yourself:

- with **love**, not judgement
- with **curiosity**, not criticism
- with **compassion**, not control.

You can choose to stop fixing – and start honouring.

Because everything you seek – more energy, deeper purpose, lasting impact – starts here.

Not with doing more. But with belonging more – to yourself.

This isn't a one-time change. It's a lifelong practice. A sacred return to what's always been true:

- That you are allowed to feel.

- You are allowed to pause.
- You are allowed to trust the quiet knowing within you.

And when you do…
You begin to lead not from fear, but from **respect**.
Not from urgency, but from **truth**.
Not from depletion, but from **love**.
And that changes everything.

So, as you close this book, my invitation is simple:
treat your body as if your life depends on it.
Because it does.
And you are worth every moment of care it takes to come home to yourself.

With deep respect, compassion, and gratitude – for you, and for the body that's carried you this far,

— **Dr Valerie Johnston-Dugamin**

To every BODY
that's been silenced, sidelined, or sacrificed:
This is your time –
to be heard,
to be honoured,
to be loved,
and to come home again.

Toolkit + next steps

> *A practical path forward*

You've completed the journey through the OsteoLife LUCKY System. But your real transformation happens now – when you begin living what you've learnt.

This section is here to support that process.

It's not about adding more to your plate. It's about helping you remember what matters when life gets busy again.

The tools below are designed to be revisited – imperfectly, intuitively, and in your own time.

The OsteoLife LUCKY Toolkit

L – Listen

Tool: The TUNE-IN Map
A guided practice to notice what your body is telling you, without judgement.

U – Understand

Tool: The DECODE Map

Track patterns, triggers, and messages over time with curiosity, not control.

C – Connect

Tool: The CONTEXT Map
Identify what nourishes you and what depletes you – physically, emotionally, environmentally.

K – Kindness

Tool: The STAY Map
Build micro-rituals that honour your real life, not your ideal one.

Y – You take action

Tool: The ACTION Map
Implement one respectful shift at a time – with space to test, reflect, and adjust.

Women in leadership

Tool: The ALIGN Map
Reset daily by returning to your body before you lead others.

How to use this toolkit

- **Return to what's relevant.** You don't need to use every tool at once. Start where you are.

- **Build your rhythm.** Use the maps and check-ins to create sustainable rituals. Make them yours.
- **Track your patterns.** Not to fix yourself – but to understand yourself more deeply.
- **Revisit without guilt.** If you drift away from the tools, come back. They're here when you need them.

Your next steps

1. **Choose one chapter to return to this week.**
   Highlight one insight that stood out – and reflect on why it matters to you now.

2. **Print or save your favourite tool from the LUCKY Toolkit.**
   Keep it visible. Let it ground you in action without overwhelm.

3. **Share what you've learnt.**
   Discuss it with someone you trust – a friend, colleague, or practitioner. Speaking it out loud makes it real.

4. **Create a reminder.**
   Write a note on your mirror. Or a phrase on your phone wallpaper. Something that reconnects you to your body each day.

Final invitation

There is no perfect way to do this work.
There is only your way.
And every time you return to yourself – even for a breath – you are doing enough.

The OsteoLife LUCKY System isn't a test to pass. It's a map to return to, again and again, as you grow.

Let this be your reminder:

You don't need to push through.
You're allowed to pause.
You're allowed to honour your body.
And you're allowed to live from that place.

OsteoLife LUCKY Toolkit worksheets

> Your practice pages for reconnection

Use these worksheets as check-ins, resets, or regular rituals. Repetition builds trust. Simplicity builds momentum.

Print them. Post them. And return as often as needed.

Chapter 2: Listen – TUNE-IN Map worksheet

Prompts:
- What physical sensation do I notice right now?
- Where is it located?
- If it had a voice, what would it say?
- What does it need from me in this moment?

_____

_____

_____

_____

_____

Chapter 3: DECODE Map worksheet

Track the pattern, not just the problem.

Date	
Symptom/Discomfort	
What was happening before?	
What emotion is present?	
My response	
Insight	

_____

_____

_____

_____

_____

_____

Chapter 4: CONTEXT Map worksheet

Identify what nourishes and what drains.

What nourishes me? (people, places, habits)	What depletes me? (triggers, drains, obligations)

Follow with:
- What do I want to do more of?
- What boundary needs attention?

_____

_____

_____

_____

Chapter 5: STAY Map worksheet

S – **Soften:** Where can I release effort?
T – **Tend:** What do I need to care for today?
A – **Allow:** What emotion or truth needs space?
Y – **Yield:** What can I let go of or delay?

Chapter 6: ACTION Map worksheet

Define one small, respectful shift.

- What feels off or disconnected right now?
- What is one small change I can try?
- How will I know it's working (signal from body)?
- When will I check in with myself?

_____

_____

_____

_____

_____

_____

Chapter 7: ALIGN Map worksheet

Your daily reset for whole-body leadership.

- **Acknowledge:** What do I feel?
- **Locate:** Where is it in my body?
- **Inquire:** What might it be asking for?
- **Ground:** How will I reset? (breath, pause, move)
- **Navigate:** What's one aligned next step?

_____

_____

_____

_____

_____

_____

_____

_____

Space for daily entry or checklist

Reminder: These tools are not about perfection. They're about presence. Return whenever you need to reconnect.

Your body remembers. Let it guide you home.

www.ingramcontent.com/pod-product-compliance
Lightning Source LLC
Chambersburg PA
CBHW071243070526
44583CB00017B/2305